The Unexpressed Veil

Finding My Voice

Freda N. Smith

Self-Published by Freda N. Smith
Riverview, Florida

THE LIBRARY OF CONGRESS HAS CATALOGED THE
PAPERBACK
BOOK EDITION

AS FOLLOWS:

Smith, Freda N.
The Unexpressed Veil: Finding My Voice / Freda N. Smith

Paperback Book Publication
Printed in the United States of America by CreateSpace.com
Edited by
Annette Delisle, David Hill & Kimberly J. James
Designed by Kimberly J. James

ISBN 13:978-0-692-67510-6

Contact: UNEXPRESSEDVEIL@GMAIL.COM

CONTENTS

Acknowledgments

Introduction

Foreword

Disclaimer

ACKNOWLEDGMENTS

The completion of this book has been made possible through the love and guidance of some very important people in my life which I have to personally acknowledge.

To the one that planted the seed for this book to be written, Diana Lynn Gaddey. I will forever be grateful for the release of the prophetic word that God spoke through you at the Spaghetti Warehouse in Tampa, Florida for me to write a book. The seed was sown by the Holy Spirit and you, along with Annette Delisle, continued to water and nurture me through the process until it became a reality.

To my Pastor, Jomo Cousins thank you for providing a place of emotional healing and guidance through the ministry of Love First Christian Center. You gave me a word from the Lord when I came to the altar that was the catalyst in helping me to "let go" of the pain from my marriage and the courage to live again.

To my friend, my sister in Christ and my boss, Traci Michelle McDowell. You didn't even know it, but the first chapter of this book was written at your kitchen table. Thank you for your generosity of spirit in allowing me to use my "downtime" to work on my personal growth and spiritual enrichment. I will always remember you.

Annette Delisle, not only did you hold me accountable to complete what God had started, but you coached me through the process by taking a personal commitment of your time to edit the first draft of my manuscript. I am humbly honored and grateful to call you my friend and I thank you for every word of encouragement.

To the most extraordinary bible teacher I know, Minister David Hill. I am grateful for the day the Lord allowed us to cross paths. You have been instrumental in my spiritual development and have proven yourself to be a faithful friend and confidant. Thank you for the many hours you dedicated in the editing of the final version of this manuscript. Thank you for always reminding me of the greatness within and your desire to see me reach my full potential.

To my extraordinarily gifted niece, Kimberly James. Thank you for having the courage to write your story which gave me the confidence to write my own. Thank you for using your gifts and talents for writing, editing, organizing, graphics and a personal commitment of many hours in revising, editing and bring my story to life through the publishing of this manuscript. You conveyed what needed to be done and walked me through the entire process. I love you so much and I look forward to the many projects God will connect us to.

I wish to thank all the people in my life who gave me something to write about. You don't have a testimony unless you go through the test. This story is because of you, whether it was good or bad, whether a positive or negative end result, it all had to happen and I am grateful for every life lesson I learned along the way.

Finally, I give honor where honor is due. Thank you Father for giving me the courage and the inspiration of the Holy Spirit to write every word contained herein. For holding me close through the many nights I wrote, as the tears ran down my face. For pushing me to finish, when there were many times I was afraid of the backlash that could come from telling the whole truth. But most importantly, for loving me unconditionally and always reminding me that I have never been alone.

INTRODUCTION

As we progress through life, every word, page and chapter of our lives is being uniquely created by the thoughts and plans of a Loving God to bring us to our expected end; to fulfill the assignment that He has for each of us. Why? ...because we all have a story to tell and those stories are birthed through our life experiences, which then create our testimonies - should we choose to acknowledge the source, the purpose and the lesson.

God has walked me through a troubled childhood, a painful and oftentimes lonely introduction to becoming an adult and an unexpected spiritual awakening. How awesome is it, that He would use all my experiences to birth this book that was always inside of me, but I didn't have the courage until now to express in words?

I can recall a time when I jokingly said to someone, "Wow, I could write a book about this family and it would be a best seller." Who knows, that could have been a prophetic declaration or a dream that God placed in me for such a time as this. May the Spirit of Esther rise up in me to set those that are in bondage free!

I invite you to follow me through the pages of this book to discover, learn and gain wisdom and insight from the process God used to restore my voice and remove the "veil", which is my testimony. When the Holy Spirit gave me the title for this book, I did not have an understanding of what it meant. After researching the word veil, this is what I discovered. A veil can be defined as something that is used to hide, cover up or conceal. It can protect the power that is on the inside from that which is on the outside. My testimony, which has been unspoken and masked for so long, God is now uncovering and calling me to release it because of the power it holds to set others free. No more secrets and no more hiding. The Word declares, "We are made over comers by the blood of the Lamb and the word of our testimony." (Revelation 12:11)

As you take this journey with me, my prayer is that you connect with something I've shared. Something that speaks to a situation(s) that you are experiencing to bring you hope, peace and freedom in knowing that if God delivered, healed and restored me, He can surely do the same for you. The Word says, "Our steps are ordered by the Lord". (Psalm 37:23) Nothing in our lives just happens. Every step in life is allowed or divinely orchestrated by a loving and faithful God (the good and the bad) to bring us to where He wants us to be. In the words of Tim Storey, "Our lives have already been spoken over by God." This will give you a different perspective on the challenges that you face in life.

Our life story has already been written by the hands of an Almighty, All Knowing God, and all we have to do is exercise our faith by taking one step at a time and discern when it's time to turn the page!

Don't allow yourself to be stuck in a mediocre life. Don't be burdened with the baggage and distress from your past. It's time to let the past be the past, breathe deep and Let Go!

Lord, I'm being completely obedient to you and trusting that this book will get into the hands of whomever you intended. In fear of the unknown, I write the *Unexpressed Veil*, because you said, "Tell your story!"

FOREWORD

"The Unexpressed Veil" is a literary gold mine that offers the reader an opportunity to share very intimate and very candid "nuggets" of a period of time in life behind the veil of silence and suffering. A life that was a demonstration of the slow, painful evolution and maturation of an awesome present-day tried and true Christian. We see the PAIN of the experiences, the PROCESSS of the transformation and the PROMOTION that includes the DELIVERANCE, which will *"restore to you the years that the locust hath eaten."* The transformation that will be witnessed within these pages has produced a new creation in Christ Jesus.

"The Unexpressed Veil" chronicles the epic and total spiritual metamorphosis of the very intimately transparent experiences that transformed this "caterpillar" into a beautiful spiritual "butterfly".

One of the most obvious attributes that one gleans from this book is the amount of courage required to have the motivation and obedience to share this life's journey, to this point. It is an effort to minister to and strengthen others that have experienced this magnitude of pain and the head winds of despair. The reader is granted the occasion to share in the deliverance of a committed life that was moved from victim to victor.

There is a "natural" veil that is full of fault, failure and futility that is pure bondage. Thank God for the "spiritual" veil that is available to the worshipper that allows access to the fullness of righteousness, restoration and redemption.

God shared this with Moses, *"And you shall hang the veil from the clasps. Then you shall bring the ark of the Testimony in there, behind the veil.* **_The veil_** *shall be* **_a divider for you between the holy place and the Most Holy_***"* (Exodus 26:33). Let us choose wisely.

David Hill

Associate Pastor
First Baptist Church of Progress Village
Tampa, Florida

DISCLAIMER

This is my true story. However, due to the sensitive nature of the topics being addressed, some of the names have been changed to protect the identities and privacy of the parties involved.

CHAPTER 1
In the Beginning

I was born and raised in Fairfax, Virginia; the thirteenth child of a total of nineteen children; twelve brothers and six sisters. I am proud to say that each one is uniquely gifted and talented in his/her own way. A perfect family we are not, but survivors, yes we are! We have each experienced our share of challenges and done things we wish we could take back. Overall, I see myself as extremely blessed and I'm very proud of each of them; the men and women they have become is in spite of enduring all kinds of hardship, pain and disappointment.

My father was one of twelve and my mother one of seven siblings. I guess they were destined to be fruitful. We lived in a four-bedroom Cape Cod style home with one bathroom and an unfinished basement (which was used as a play area and for me - an escape route as a teenager). When the home was completed, it was adequate space for the existing occupants; four boys and two girls. Mama must have felt a sense of pride and excitement to be in a brand new home. Although they were very young (at least one year apart in age for some), my siblings had to be pretty excited as well to have their own home, after living on my grandparent's farm in a two room house.

Mama was an attractive woman with a small frame and beautiful long hair in her early years. Prior to marriage, she enjoyed outings with her sisters whenever she had an opportunity. She was devoted to her parents until their death. When she met daddy, she said he was very handsome and quite a talker. He came from a large family that she considered to be well off, compared to her own. Daddy's family owned their farm and home in Vienna, Virginia. Her parents worked in the home of a well to do Caucasian family in the City of Fairfax, where she was born and raised. Granddad was the chauffer and grandma was the maid.

Mama told me that she thought marrying daddy would give her an opportunity for a better way of life. She said, Grandma was never fond of him and for that reason did not often visit her home, although she lived on the same street. Apparently grandma was jealous of his family because of what she presumed they had. Mama adored her father. Granddad was a sweet and gentle soul but very quiet and bless his heart, he is what we called "henpecked" – bullied or intimidated by one's wife. In sharing some of her childhood with me, mama once told me, "I know my daddy loved me, but I never felt my mother's love." By her account, she lived the "Cinderella life." She said that she did the majority of the housework, so I can understand why she felt getting married would be a way of escape. So, I guess that would have made daddy her "Prince Charming."

THE UNEXPRESSED VEIL

When they married, she moved from her parent's home to his parent's home on the farm, with fruit trees and a long driveway lined with grapevines. The property was lush with green grass and in the middle of the front yard was a huge cow lick. I have to admit, I licked it myself a few times out of curiosity. The main house reminded me of a smaller version of the house depicted in the movie, "Color Purple," tin roof and all.

They moved into the little house that was directly beside the main house. Mama gave birth to her first four children in that little two room house. Fortunately for them, living on the farm kept them from experiencing hunger and lack, as we did. Wasting food was not tolerated. My grandmother would always say, "Take what you want but eat everything you put on your plate". Almost every Sunday, grandma's house was the meeting place for all the family to gather. Daddy's sisters and brothers would come with their families. They would sit around talking while the kids ran around. Those were great times. My paternal grandfather had already passed before I was born, so I have no memory of him, but the others shared great memories. He was described as a stern man, but very kind and hardworking.

As a little girl, I had such fun spending time at that old farmhouse. I recall watching my grandmother kill chickens in the front yard and helping her to churn butter at the same time watching my dad and uncles preparing to slaughter the bulls. For me, those really were the good old days; a happier time.

I enjoyed sitting around all the elders and listening to their stories and jokes and yes sometimes even exaggerated truths.

Mama spoke well of most of daddy's family. Grandma and Granddad were very kind to her and Grandma Smith taught her a great deal about running a home. She loved being on the farm, but quickly learned what it meant to be married but feel completely alone.

When they moved to Fairfax, mama was pregnant with her fifth child. Daddy worked for a grocery store at the time, so things were not as bad for them or the additional siblings that continued to come. Despite the loneliness, mama seemed to have fairly pleasant memories of her life on the farm. She was probably treated better by Grandma Smith than she was by her own mother. Grandma Smith taught her how to cook and she was an excellent cook.

Eventually that beautiful farm and the rich heritage that came with it were sold. My grandmother moved into the home that she and my uncle had my father build for them. I learned many years after the deaths of both my grandmother and uncle that it was my grandmother's intent for my dad to live in this home with his family. She had him build it the way he wanted for that purpose. It was a beautiful, well-built brick home in Vienna, Virginia that sat on a huge piece of property. She even had him build a garage that was to be used for his carpentry tools. It had a large front porch, large dining and living room area and a huge basement. Yes, this home would have more than sufficed to raise his children. In hindsight, I can't say any of us would have traded living on School Street for anything, so I suppose it all worked out the way it was intended.

Daddy was a very handsome, strong and opinionated man. He had a need to be right about everything. I didn't realize it as a young girl, but he was for sure a "mama's boy." Daddy spent a lot of time with his mom and other family members; especially his sisters. They all seemed to dote over him, being the youngest of the siblings. According to mama, his father would often get angry with grandma for protecting and coddling him. When both of his parents died, the siblings continued in that behavior. Daddy worked in a bakery, for the post office and eventually as a self-employed carpenter. Although he didn't have trouble finding work and earning money, the responsibility of providing for his wife and family was not on his priority list, likely a consequence of being spoiled by his mother and older siblings. Therefore, his family was always coming to his rescue. He was also not one for spending time at home. He spent a great deal of time in the streets or visiting other people's homes, to my mother's dismay. He was a hard worker and extremely intelligent and gifted in many areas. Unfortunately, it did not benefit his wife and or children.

Our neighborhood was an all-black community and most of our neighbors were relatives. "School Street" was more of an identity than a street name. The house was nestled on a huge lot with beautiful oak trees and a well maintained lawn with all types of foliage, plants and flowers lovingly planted by my mom's well-worn hands. Mama loved being outside where she could watch the people come and go, watch her grandchildren play, and of course, get updates on the neighborhood gossip every now and again.

By the time I came along, our house was "worn" from years of activity from the first batch of kids (my twelve older siblings), but it was still a home built by the hands of both my father and mother, while she was pregnant. Now that's a pioneer woman if I ever saw one. Mama took great care in keeping up her modest home; planting flowers was a pleasure and a joy for her. She always stressed to us the importance of taking care of what we have. We didn't have much in the way of material things, but we did have a roof over our heads, which she kept spotless. I remember mama getting us girls up at the crack of dawn to clean while she was in the yard raking and sweeping up leaves and acorns. We could always tell when she was up and moving because of the strong scent of Clorox bleach permeating throughout the house.

In our household, there was no such thing as sleeping-in. My parents arose early and we were raised to do the same. Daddy was generally gone by the time the kids got up, but mama was always there. In many ways, it seemed like we were raised in a one parent home. On Saturday mornings, we did get to enjoy some cereal while watching cartoons. Most of the time, breakfast consisted of cereal, but not the kind most kids enjoyed eating. We ate what was available and on sale, but every now and again, it was a real treat to enjoy our family favorites, "Captain Crunch" or mama's pancakes.

Because of the number of us in the home, mama would stand at the stove for long periods of time with her hand on her hip, making a pile of pancakes. Some of us liked them a little on the dark side, while others didn't care how they came out as long as we got to eat them all. Sometimes we had butter and syrup and other times, we just had one or the other. Whatever she had in the house, she created a meal to feed her brood of children.

By their own acknowledgement, life had not been easy for either of my parents or African Americans in general at that time, and the struggles they faced were very real. My dad was not a lazy man by any means. He was never without a job, but we were always lacking in finances. For a brief time, to have money to feed her children and to take care of other expenses, mama worked cleaning apartments. When that was no longer feasible, she took on odd jobs, cleaning and washing and being a babysitter for some of the single moms in the community.

Before the younger bunch came along, both mama and daddy were actively involved in the Civil Rights Movement. Daddy was very passionate about standing up for the fair treatment of African American children in the Fairfax County School System, and became a respected voice in our community about education in general. If there was a cause, or a fight, he was all in it. Most government officials in City Hall, as well as our elementary school administrators knew the name Stanley Smith, either because of his outspoken personality, his reputation as a quality builder, or most often because of the number of children he had.

Despite his public efforts, education was never a high priority among the children in our family. We were expected to do well, but if we didn't that was on us. I felt that the benefit of going to school was to get away from my dysfunctional home environment and the assurance of having at least two hot meals per day. Depending on the season, school was also a place to be warm or stay cool. At school, I was able to forget about the environment at home and pretend I had a different life. At times, I had to go to school on an empty stomach, without school supplies, and without lunch money. With that amount of stress, it was difficult, if not impossible, to focus on learning.

I will be forever grateful for the kindness and love I received from one of my childhood friends, Lois Jackson. She not only helped me with my school work, but many times she fed me as well. She used to ask me, "Freda, how is it that your parents allow you to miss so many days from school?" She had no idea of the type of issues I dealt with at home. There were numerous reasons that I stayed home. There were times that I stayed home because mama needed help, or I didn't have feminine products to get me through the day, or as I mentioned previously, I often didn't have school supplies to complete a project or assignment that was due.

Every year, as we returned to school, each one of us had a teacher that had taught an older sibling. Their comment was always, "You must be one of the Smith kids. Are you such and such's sister?" My response was, "yes I am and don't expect me to be as smart as they were!" I said that to myself because I always followed after two of my brothers that were very intelligent and naturally gifted in many areas. I, on the other hand, hated school and didn't enjoy any subject other than Gym, History and English. I got hooked on History in High School because it was the first time that I was taught about Black History. Of course that was only one month each year, but I loved learning about my heritage.

Out of a desire for a different life than what we were living, there was a time when my little brother and I pretended that our favorite uncle was actually our Father. I dreamed of living in a beautiful home, like those of my school friends. A home where I'd be greeted with love and be provided for by parents who were interested in me and what was going on in my life. That was not my reality, I am sad to say. We knew mama loved us by the daily sacrifices she made, but neither my mother nor my father were equipped to create a loving and nurturing home environment, conducive to raising emotionally healthy children. Not because they didn't want to, but because they never had that example mirrored before them. I've accepted that you can't give what you've never had.

As I began to see our family life for what it was, I felt badly for my brothers. The girls, although mama didn't have much individual time for us, was always there and we had plenty of opportunities to learn from her. My brothers, however, never had a positive image to follow in learning to be men. They never had the benefit of receiving encouragement or positive praise for anything they did. What was demonstrated before them was a man that didn't respect, or appreciate, his wife. As well as a father, who didn't always provide for his family's basic needs and didn't care for his home. My perception was that he had no time for his children; he cared more about his extended family and church than the needs of his own. He took no responsibility for his actions. These words may seem harsh, but it was OUR truth; a reality that we lived every day. But, in spite of all that, my childhood "memories" are mostly pleasant because I made a conscious decision to focus on the positive and not dwell on the negative.

Coming from such a large family, there were always relatives to visit and a house full of siblings and cousins to be entertained. I would characterize myself as being a "tom boy" growing up. I tried to do anything that I saw my brothers do. I loved being outdoors and running around with the kids. For some reason, I always had a love and appreciation for nature. I enjoyed taking walks through the woods, which was where I found peace and quiet from all the confusion of life. It is where I learned to talk to God, even though I didn't know who He was at the time.

THE UNEXPRESSED VEIL

I never took much of an interest playing with dolls and such, but my friends and I had fun playing "house" and pretending we had kids. We made dirt pies, played in the creek and climbed trees. We also played church in a make shift tree house, played at the playground or just hung out in our backyard. I was a short, stubby little kid (which earned me the nickname "nee nee"). I had long black hair, which I wore in ponytails, but to this day, my sisters would disagree with that statement - but it was true.

Growing up, I didn't have a lot of friends; for us it was all about family. I did have two best friends that I am still connected with to this day, Yvette and Samantha. Where you saw one you typically saw the other. We were thick as thieves. I really enjoyed the times I was allowed to go to their homes to play but that was few and far between. Mama was very strict when it came to raising the girls in the family. I was allowed to go away from the house, but most of the time only if one of my brother's was going to be there. To say my mom was over protective is an understatement.

My friend Samantha's parents were the best! Their father treated them to a family outing every Monday. On occasion, she was allowed to invite a friend on some of these outings. I was always beyond excited when Samantha would ask my mom if I could go with them. She trusted Samantha's parents because at one point, in their younger days, her parents lived with us (before I was born).

We had the best times visiting Luray Cavern's, a beautiful and scenic place in Virginia and best of all, we ALWAYS stopped by McDonald's on the way home. Eating at a restaurant was never something we were able to do in our family. The couple of times I recall daddy taking us out to eat was a surprise, but we were limited to one item only. You had a choice of a cheeseburger and/or French Fries… never both and forget about a drink. With Samantha's parents, you could get whatever you wanted. That was pure heaven!

I loved growing up on School Street, but in the summer months I looked forward to our outings to Grandma Smith's farm. I had a great time visiting my father's relatives. My Aunt Josie and Tippy (everybody had a nickname) were the best cooks. There was never a time that we visited them that they didn't have something cooking or baking and there were always cookies or cake for us to enjoy.

Daddy would make his rounds visiting his family which at times was not always pleasurable for mama. I think she just enjoyed being together as a family and getting out of the house. My uncles were always a hoot to be around. Some were meek and quiet; others boisterous and the best comedians I know to this day. Daddy seemed like a different person when he was around his own, always the loudest one in any conversation, with the most to say. But, everybody loved "Uncle Stanley" as he was referred to.

Aside from the family gatherings on Sunday's after church, we didn't see him much. When he was home, he was watching the news or sleeping. There wasn't a lot of interaction with either parent. Mama was busy taking care of the house; cleaning, cooking, washing and so much more. Life had never been easy for her. She went from a home life of having grown up responsibilities to being a wife and mother with a lot of responsibility and little financial stability to get it done.

We had little money for clothes and shoes. Most of us, being close in age and size, were able to share with each other. Our clothes were never new. I remember going with my mom to a thrift store in Vienna. She was able to get a few bags of clothes and shoes. I don't remember if she had to pay, or if they were given to us, but I was excited. They may have been used, but it was like new to me. On one occasion, my little brother and I, got tennis shoes. I was so excited to have those shoes. For me, those shoes were everything. I couldn't wait to try them out. I put those shoes on and like "Forrest Gump," I ran like the wind.

Because money was always an issue, we didn't have many toys, but that didn't stop us. My brothers and their friends were creative and talented in making what our parents couldn't afford to purchase. When we didn't have bikes, we made stick horses. We also created obstacle courses in the yard and enjoyed simple pleasures like jumping in freshly raked leaves or swinging from makeshift swings attached to the big Oak Trees in the yard. In the winter months, my personal favorite was sleigh riding on trash bags or inner tubes on the streets or down the hills in the neighborhood. Being poor will bring out your creativity and gifts.

Whatever time of the year, our back yard was always filled with neighborhood kids. My friends would stop at our house after school looking to see if mama had baked anything that day. Mama loved to bake when she had the resources. She baked cakes, cookies, pies and her homemade bread was always a favorite. Having all the kids around was never a problem for my mom because she loved kids, but she was not one to have them in her home. She was good as long as we stayed outside to play.

The summer months were always the best for us kids. There was always plenty of activity on our street. People would come to "School Street" from neighboring communities to hang out, listen to music, gamble or play horse shoes. I think my mom enjoyed summer the most. She could sit out in the yard under the big oak tree and just watch the people and talk with neighbors and friends. People would drive or walk by and if they saw her sitting there, they would stop in to chat or just call out, "Hey Ms. Nettie." Mama was the type of person that was welcoming and kind to (most) people in the community and never judged them for their behaviors or way of life; how could she? Her children were not perfect either.

The people in our community were very talented in sports. We had a local softball team and the highlight of the summer was gathering at the local elementary school to watch the games. The kids played in the playground and the grownups enjoyed sitting around smoking, drinking and sharing tall tales. We had some real characters in our neighborhood. To this day, most of those in my family carry memories from growing up on that street that they will cherish for a lifetime. Those were the best of times and the worst of times all rolled up in one.

Much can be said about our childhood on School Street. If you asked each of us about that period, you would probably get a completely different viewpoint. Since this is my story, I'm telling it from what I remember and my personal perspective.

As my older brothers grew up, some of them began working alongside my dad in his carpentry business. They often butted heads because they were all "know it all's" just like him. They all possessed the same gifting in carpentry, masonry and dry wall work. The most frustrating thing for them was being left on a jobsite, working themselves to the bone and not being compensated. My dad had a habit of doing work for people either for free or for much less than he should have. That may have been okay for him, but my brothers were not interested in working for free or less than fair wages.

Neither he, nor my brother's took full advantage of their gifts and talents. With the wealth of talent and intellect we all possessed, our family could have and should have had successful businesses that would have provided a legacy for our children and generations to come. My father continued to build through the years without my brothers, but it never provided a consistent income to provide for his family. We were always barely getting by and that was only because my mom started taking care of neighborhood children and eventually, my older siblings took on the responsibility when needed of providing for the basic care of the younger kids.

From the outside looking in, it appeared that my mom's days and nights were consumed by raising kids (her own, grandchildren and neighbors). I personally, wouldn't have wished that on my worst enemy, but oddly enough, my mom seemed to enjoy the kids, the noise and the constant flow of friends and neighbors that always stopped in to visit her. I think it helped to fill the void in her heart left by a husband who chose not to be present. She surrounded herself with grandkids that she knew adored her and needed her and she had few relationships outside of family.

Mama enjoyed going out with one of my sisters-in-law to play bingo and cards. That was her escape and I'm glad she had it, because I also remember as a child, watching my mom staring out the window or sitting in the front yard by the tree, burning trash to keep the bugs away while quietly looking for my dad's car to come down the street. It never did. My dad would leave before daybreak and we wouldn't see him until after the sun went down, if then. I'm sure she didn't realize it at the time, but a root of bitterness was rising up towards my father and consequently, her responses to life were teaching her children to endure and suffer in silence rather than open their mouths and speak.

My family life was not always pleasant, but one thing was a constant in our lives. Going to church on Sunday morning. If we didn't see daddy any other time, it was a given that we would all be together at church on Sunday. In our house, going to church was not an option (thank God for that example). I didn't complain too much because I saw it as an opportunity to go out as a family and visit my dad's family. Being such a prideful man, daddy always showed off his kids around his family and friends. At home it was a much different story. We never heard words of encouragement or words at all for that matter, unless it was to bring correction. Showing any type of affection was definitely not his way. That is... until his grandchildren came along. When my sister, Amber gave birth to Danielle, she became the object of his affection. He loved showing her off. I'd never seen that side of him. I guess over the years; he began to appreciate his family. The love he didn't express to his own children, he made up for in loving his grandchildren.

If we could just make it through the service, we knew the next stop was grandma's house or one of our aunts. Like my mother, they always had plenty of baked treats for us to enjoy. In spite of all the hardships, rejection, loneliness and loss my mom experienced ALL her life, I think she would say her greatest achievement in life was "raising her children" the best way she knew how and she did that with great pride. With everything that we lacked, my mother had a gift of making something out of nothing – especially a meal.

To be as poor as we were, we always seemed to have more than enough during the holidays. I suppose that was from the contributions provided by all that came. Gathering during special holidays like Thanksgiving and Christmas was the best. We always assembled together at someone's home; all 30 of us (including the kids).

We "cut-up" on each other and laughed about the good old days. We danced, sang and ate until we were ready to burst! My older siblings always made sure we were not neglected at Christmas. My two oldest sisters, Carolyn and Linda (Lin) in particular were our saving grace many times. They did what they could to help mama financially. Sometimes, things got so difficult that my dad's brothers would come and bring my mom a "love offering" to help. I wish they had taken the approach to counsel their brother on the meaning of providing for family vs. allowing others to assume the responsibility. Although it was a blessing, I could see my mom was a little ashamed to accept what was being given.

Family should always be there to help one another in times of need, but it should never be the sole burden of the older siblings. That's what happened with Carolyn and Lin. They had to take on the role of mother and father to all the younger siblings at a time when they were trying to build their own lives and raise their own children.

One winter, the house was so cold the gold fish froze in the tank. By my brother's account, they froze with their mouths open. We had many laughs over that in the years that followed. We went a few days with no heat. The only thing to keep us warm was the clothes on our backs and each other. As a last resort, my mother contacted my sister-in-law and made arrangements for us to come to her house. There had been a very heavy snow fall, so traveling by car (which we didn't have anyway) was not possible. Mama got us all together and we set out on foot, through several feet of snow to get to the main road. The image must have been startling to our neighbors to see my mom and all her kids trailing behind her through the snow. When we approached the top of the hill, there was my dad. He was standing out on the street talking to one of the neighbors who we lovingly called "Uncle Jake." In my young mind I thought to myself, "why is daddy here instead of being home with us?" That had to be terribly embarrassing for mama and should have been for my dad. We laugh about these experiences today, because what didn't kill us surely made us stronger.

God seemed to always provide a safety net through someone for us. When things were difficult at home, most of us had a place to run to for safety, provision or just peace. That was the benefit in growing up in a small community where most people were relatives or just amazing friends. My younger sisters and some of my brothers were blessed in that way. We used survival skills we didn't know we had. I will always be grateful for the family's God placed in our lives.

I applaud my brothers and sisters that had children. They made sure their children did not repeat the pattern of poverty. Everyone, to the extent they could, worked hard to provide for their children because they had experienced the sting of poverty growing up. So, all things do work together for good because along the way God was building character even through our pain.

Our family endured extremely difficult times, but by the Grace of God we survived. It's strange to me, but when I look back at my childhood, my focus is not on what we didn't have. My memory is flooded by all the great fun we shared as siblings and with relatives and friends.

CHAPTER 2
Silence of the Lamb
Generational Curses

For my parents, the concept of family was supposed to be a source of joy, laughter and pride. Historically, my dad was born into a family that had been marred by the effects of slavery, racism and what many in their generation referred to as a "code of silence." I believe my mom's family had their share of issues as well, but I wasn't as connected to them as I was my father's family. Through an extensive undertaking into the "Smith" family history, by one of my nieces, things were uncovered that helped me to make sense of a secret that I'd been holding onto for years. I can only explain it as what I have come to understand to be... a Generational Curse. According to research conducted by my niece, Kimberly James in writing her book, "Running on G", and a most incredible work of genealogical research conducted by my niece, Lisa Noel, they discovered the following about our family history and where it all began. In Kim's words they discovered many things.

"The generational curse began with the slave master of our ancestor, Ann Lucas. According to the history, Mr. William Presgraves enslaved and raped our great, great, great, great, great grandmother Ann Lucas, fathering several of her kids and continued sexual relationships with her and his daughters until she was emancipated. He then made a deal to marry her off to a Smith man and gave him a piece of property to build a home in exchange for keeping the secret of his paternity. This starting the cycle of incest and sexual immorality in our family line. I only knew of his name and my aunt Linda shared stories that she used to hear from grandma that his wife, Mary used to tie Grandma Lucas to a tree and beat her (aware of the liberties that her husband took with Grandma Lucas." My niece Lisa, the family historian, later confirmed the validity of those stories.

The bible refers to a <u>Generational Curse</u> as iniquities and sin that is passed down from one generation to another as is depicted in the following scripture(s): (**<u>Exodus 20:5; 34:7; Numbers 14:18; Deuteronomy 5:9</u>**).

My grandfather was a product of the ugliness of slavery. He was a mulatto and was very ashamed and angered most of his adult life, according to conversations that he'd shared with my father.

I never knew Granddaddy Smith but I heard many stories of the type of person that he was and wished I'd had the opportunity to know him. I did however, have an opportunity to know my Grandma Smith. The Smith clan were a proud people but very dedicated to their parents and one another.

Mama shared with me that before grandma died, she apologized to her for not raising my dad to be a man and take responsibility for his family. She acknowledged that she had sheltered him as the youngest of her children, which in her words ruined, him as a man.

It was the exact opposite in my mom's family. I never saw the personal closeness or commitment, but they were a fun bunch. My mom's father was my favorite. He was a quiet, gentle and loving man. Her parents lived on the same street, not far from our home. I so enjoyed spending time with my grandfather in the front yard. I would sit with him for hours just listening to him talk. I think that was the beginning of my heart of compassion for the elderly.

My grandmother seemed to take great issue with him spending time with me, but she had issue with all of mama's kids for some reason. She would send me home when she felt I had been there long enough and my grandfather just went along with whatever she said. I never respected her much, because of how I saw her treat him and my mom. In their later years, and I'm sure before then, my mom was always very loyal to her parents. Especially to her dad. I watched her care for her father, as he began to experience health issues. He was always so appreciative of everything she did but grandma never showed or expressed her appreciation.

She had certainly lived a Cinderella life. In fact, later in life, she told me that she never felt loved by her mother and lived her entire life being fearful about everything. I have found in my life, that if you look at a person's history, you'll discover the "whys" to their personality and responses to life. I know my mom loved her parents and siblings, but I don't believe love was an emotion expressed and felt in their household.

In my distressed childhood, I remember those times of isolation. I would sit on my front porch reading my bible, running or taking long walks through the woods pondering the many questions I had about life. I had a longing to know who God really was. My childhood experiences were the catalyst for giving me a desire to know God and the foundation to return to when I strayed. I remember being such a deep thinker. The basic answers just didn't seem to go deep enough for me. I wanted to know who He was and I needed to make sense of why things were happening to me. In some ways, that was probably my escape from reality at the time.

I was living in a house full of children that were void of love, affection and positive attention. Most of us lacked self-esteem and confidence. In my mom's defense, (not that she needs one), she was overwhelmed with life trying to raise so many children without the support, love or assistance from her husband. Not to mention the emotional pain she carried in silence.

I came to understand as an adult, going through my own emotional healing, that your parents cannot give you something they've never had. All they know is what was mirrored before them as children. Understanding this concept completely freed me from my disappointment in my parents and allowed me to forgive and accept them for who they were.

I learned to love them unconditionally and forgive them completely. Even though my father was never around, I always tried to do things that would make him proud of me. I was so excited when he took me to his jobsites in the summer months. In those times, it seemed you had his complete attention and he seemed proud to call you his own. For all my siblings, I wish we could have experienced that throughout our upbringing. We may have been much better adults.

I have since learned the long lasting effect and impact that childhood experiences have on your adult life and every relationship. We all have baggage and scars resulting from unresolved and most often than not, unspoken acts/experiences endured in our childhood. Those things were too painful, embarrassing or shameful to discuss with anyone, thus enabling the "code of silence." All this leads to a dysfunctional lifestyle until we have the courage to speak out and get real with ourselves. Pastor Paula White used to say, "You cannot conquer what you do not confront; you cannot confront what you do not identify." Until the darkness is exposed to the light, it will always be a weapon of Satan to keep you in bondage, torment, fear, shame and guilt.

I was about ten or eleven years old when I recall the first of multiple experiences of molestation at the hands of family members and neighbors.

Our doors were never locked in those days. My mom often allowed people to stay in our home, who needed a temporary place to live. Consequently, the girls became "open prey" to anyone who came in.

I hated to see the night come because you never knew who was going to be creeping around. My family secret was Molestation! There, I said it aloud. I can't even tell you as I came to this part of the book, how hard it was for me to write that word. I had to research the definition before I became comfortable using the terminology to describe our family curse. Based on what I found, it is an accurate reflection of what many of my female relatives and I experienced:

Molestation

The crime of sexual acts with children up to the age of 18; including touching of private parts, exposure of genitalia and rape. Molestation also applies to incest by a relationship with a minor family member, and any unwanted sexual acts with adults short of rape.

I was raped twice; once as a teenager by a family member and again as an adult by a distant cousin. Those were my two worst experiences. As a result, I was imprisoned by what has been a life long struggle with male relationships, fear of speaking out, guilt, shame, low self-esteem, poor body image and the constant thought of never being good enough or deserving of anything. Wow, that's a mouth full of issues!

THE UNEXPRESSED VEIL

I used to envy my friends thinking their home life had to be far better than mine. They never missed a meal; came home to a cold house; lights off; no phone or the possibility of someone outside the family sleeping on the floor on any given night. I did occasionally enjoy quiet moments in my room, which I shared with four other sisters.

When had this vileness taken residence in our home? When God gave me the courage to face my childhood past, it was clear to me that it wasn't anything new and didn't begin in our home but in our family line.

When it began with me, it never occurred to me that I wasn't the only one, until I witnessed it happening to an older sister, followed by the confession of my younger sisters Patrice, Amber, Beth and a couple of my niece's, years later. I was sickened by it, but I never had the courage to ask any of them who their abusers were. Eventually, I was relieved to know that not all the males in the family were guilty of these acts. I do not, and will never, find it necessary to reveal the names of those that abused my sisters, my nieces and me.

I recall watching the movie, "The Color Purple" as an adult. Oprah Winfrey's character, Sophia was talking with Celie and she made the statement, *"A girl child ain't safe in a house of men."* Oh, how true that was I thought, recalling my own acquaintance with this ugliness. I remember thinking to myself, "Wow that happens for real with other families." Then I started to wonder if this was only prevalent in black families or did it happen to white families as well. I discovered later, that this "spirit" was not at all color blind and gained strength because of the shame it brought. People, to this day remain silent, still suffering this quiet shame. It is too disgusting and ugly to verbalize to anyone.... Not even to God! I know that sounds crazy, right? ...but none the less, it was true for me. I saw and experienced a lot and I suffered emotionally and physically, but never spoke a word in those early years.

As I said, it started around the age of ten or eleven, with fondling. With the exception of the one instance of rape, they were generally smart enough to protect themselves. They never attempted to vaginally penetrate me. There was however, an attempt at anal sex; again to protect himself. I did not understand what was happening to me or why. It only happened at night and I could never understand how they managed to do it so frequently, without anyone else hearing or seeing them. It was so evil and calculated, when I think about it. They never showed their faces, but I always knew who it was by their voice and with one, by the smell of his breathe. To this day, that remains etched in my memory, so much so that I can sometimes smell it and it still absolutely disgusts me.

Whenever I felt a presence, I attempted to push them away without making any noise; an unusual unspoken obligation to protect them from being caught. That has to be one of the most damaging traits of the cycle of abuse. If they were unsuccessful, I always knew they would try again sooner or later. When I witnessed what happened to my sister Cookie, I questioned if this was a normal thing, even though something in me knew it couldn't be.

The guilt and confusion came later as my body began to respond to the fondling. When that started, I was left feeling guilty and disgusted with myself. I was about fifteen or sixteen when I was raped by a family member. To my surprise, it happened during the day rather than by cover of night. He was clearly under the influence of drugs or alcohol. I don't know which it was, but by the look in his eye, I knew he was not himself.

There was no warning, he just came into my room as I was reading on my bed and forced himself onto me. That had never happened before and there was no previous assault by this individual, so it really took me by surprise. I never expected it would go that far because it was daylight and I knew people where downstairs in the house. I tried to fight him off, but to no avail. When he was finished, he just walked away like it was nothing and I was left feeling like dirty trash. Again, I never spoke of the incident.

No matter what occurred at night, when morning came, if I saw them, it was as if nothing happened. When I did encounter them, it was complete silence and sometimes not even a glance in my direction.

As a teenager, I began to experience what I call the

"side effects" of being sexually abused…
Promiscuity. My body was maturing and I
developed a curiosity about sex and the female
body. Although I never saw myself as cute or
attractive, I was catching the eye of boys and grown
men because I was well developed by the age of 10;
around the same time that I started my cycle. I went
to my mom when that happened, because I did not
know what to do. The "birds and bees" conversation
that most moms have with their young daughters
probably didn't consist of "you make your bed
hard… you lay in it." That's what I got, which was
likely the same thing her mom probably told her.
Thank goodness my sister-in-law was there in those
days and told me what I needed to know.

My first voluntary sexual experience was in my
early teens with a neighbor. (The first rape occurred
a few years later.) It certainly was not an act of
love, but rather an obligation to please. My warped
interpretation of love (that I desperately longed for)
was defined by giving myself sexually to please
others. I thought it would make me feel more grown
up to my girlfriends as if we were all competing to
be the first. I can't even explain how nasty and dirty
I felt, not to mention the guilt, knowing what my
mother would say if she found out.

That first encounter opened me up to things I could
have never prepared for. I had relations with others
after this experience and I can honestly say, not one
was ever satisfying or pleasing to me until the age
of 25. I had wasted my teenage life giving myself to
people who didn't care about me. I wondered if I

could have avoided all this had that spirit of perversion not been planted in me. Only God knows. He allowed it, so I know at some point he will use it for my good to minister to others. Everything is not God sent but it will be God used.

All of my childhood and adolescent experiences of abuse had disastrous effects on me mentally, physically and emotionally. Feelings of unworthiness, low self-esteem, poor self-image (which remains a stronghold to this day), fear, anger, and most devastating as an adult, a learned behavior of silencing my voice. I think I assumed as long as I kept quiet I would not be noticed. My silence became a means of protection.

I found the courage to face my truth after moving to Florida in 2004. I was alone with God for the first time in years and He gave me the opportunity to be cleansed from my past and start over with a new sense of purpose. To do that, I had to look myself in the mirror and allow God to draw out all the poison, darkness and shame that had almost strangled the life out of me; I had to trust God to help me bring out what I had successfully kept a secret for many years. By the grace of God, one day I sat down and began to write a family letter and sent it by mail to all my siblings and parents. Sometimes it's easier, and perhaps safer, to write rather than to speak. In any case, the result is that you rid yourself of it by exposing and releasing it to God.

My intent in writing the letter was to shed a light on what my childhood experience was like after having being a victim of molestation and rape. I knew I didn't have it in me to confront my abusers (still in protective mode), but I could no longer hide the truth. I wanted my family to be set free from this and the only way I knew to do it was to expose it.

Because God had done such a work in my heart, the most important reason for writing the letter was to let them know, I completely forgave them and I had no anger in my heart towards them. Why? Because God helped me to see that it was not them, but rather a spirit that operated through them (a generational curse) that they were completely unaware of. Once I had a clear understanding of that, I could not hold their actions against them. It was a sickness/disease that I believe was in both the Smith and the Payne family blood line. In my mind, their issues were no different than the struggles that are faced by those with addictions to alcohol, drugs, pornography, etc. You know it's wrong but you're drawn to it and driven by it. The sins of the father(s), had visited the generations. By exposing this sickness, I knew it would break the cycles and our children would be protected and they were.

It was my hope that my abusers would acknowledge and seek God's forgiveness, but I never had an expectation that they would apologize or seek my forgiveness for their inappropriate behavior. At the time that I wrote the letter or even now, I never felt it necessary to receive any acknowledgement to move forward in my life.

Although no one acknowledged their actions and/or

apologized for any wrongdoing, I knew they were remorseful and probably wished the events never took place. One of my brothers was in jail at the time. I remember speaking to him by phone. He was the only one that expressed sympathy for what I experienced. He said he had no idea that was all happening. Sometimes it's easier to deny the existence of evil rather than to confront it.

Making the decision to write that family letter was very hard, but necessary. The outcome caused the darkness to be lifted as my sisters and nieces began to open up and share their experiences. I had NO idea of the extent of the damage! The conversation stayed between the girls until finally a few of my sisters confronted my mom. She denied knowing anything or that anyone ever shared this information with her. Needless to say, it became a heated argument, somewhat out of control, but, I think it was necessary. Once it was revealed that one of my sisters was abused by one of my mom's brothers, we were fairly certain she had probably experienced the same thing in her family.

Unknowingly, mama had a way of making her daughters feel less important compared to her sons. In her mind, they could do no wrong. In that argument, I watched all of the pent up anger, frustration and disappointment come out in my sister's words towards my mom.

As I quietly observed and listened to this exchange, I thought to myself, my mom can't handle this... but they need to release it. That day, everything was brought out into the open and was forced to be resolved once and for all. From that point on, I think we all began to heal and perhaps my mom as well.

I often wondered why mama was so strict with us girls. She was so concerned about us being around boys and going out. What she didn't understand was that the trouble wasn't on the outside, but inside of our home. To this day, I don't know why I never told my mom or anyone else when it started. In some sick way, I was more concerned about embarrassing them or getting them in trouble. Again, the "code of silence" was in my DNA.

Even as I write this book, I can't tell you how much of a struggle it has been to go public. But again, it is not to bring harm or negative attention to my family, but an act of obedience to tell my story, the whole story. I understand that it's not about me, but what God wants to do in the lives of my family and those who will read this book.

Perhaps and I'm praying that in reading this book, they will repent and ask God for forgiveness. That they will be delivered and set free from this dark cloud that has had a negative effect on them. Who can say whether many of their addictions and relationship issues were born out of their unconfessed sin? Whatever you keep silent about, gives access to the enemy to continue to have control over your life.

As bad as it was, I still love those that hurt me and have never treated them any different. Even then,

God's grace did not allow me to harbor un-forgiveness towards any of them. I'm so grateful for that because, I truly love my family and wish God's best for them and their families.

I wish to offer this advice to those of you, who may have or are in an environment where "molestation" and other sexual perversions are taking place. Understand, your abuser is not evil in themselves. They are being used by a foul, perverted spirit sent by Satan to destroy you. Satan's desire, is to prevent you from becoming all God intended for you.

Yes, we all have free will, but people can be controlled by demonic forces and not be aware of it. Understanding this fact, made it easier for me to love and forgive my abusers despite their actions. Ask God to help you to forgive them, so they can be released and you can be healed.

If our abusers read this, I hope they will understand the magnitude of their actions and the why, and ask God for forgiveness and deliverance. That spirit was finally broken in our family to protect the next generation. You may have to do the same to ensure that your next generation does not live with their "daddy's" demons. Talk about it, confront it and let it go. When you grow up in this environment, it leaves you with a longing to be loved. It also opens the door for the enemy to kill, steal and destroy any hope of having a healthy loving relationship, if you don't first destroy yourself through poor choices and self-destructive behaviors. I made many, but thank God that I learned from them all.

Freda N. Smith

CHAPTER 3
When Darkness Falls
Tormenting Spirits & Depression

Having developed such a poor self-image, I was
never very outgoing. I also was very lonely and
empty until the age of twenty-four. I was introduced
to a man that was the complete opposite of myself. I
came to love this man with all my heart. There was
nothing that I wouldn't do for him. We were
completely from two different worlds. I was quiet
and reserved, with major self-esteem issues, and he
was the popular DJ from Jersey and into the night
life. He was my first romantic relationship and
consequently the one that was the hardest to break.

Over the fifteen-year relationship, (yes I know, who
does that right?). I held onto him emotionally and
we continued to have a physical relationship, when
it was convenient. I thought we were in a
relationship, but he never truly committed himself
to me. A fifteen-year booty call is what it actually
was. This relationship could best be described as a
"Soul Tie."

Definition: Soul Tie

*A soul tie can serve many functions, but in its
simplest form, it ties two souls together in the
spiritual realm. In the demonic world, unholy
soul ties can serve as bridges between two*

people to pass demonic garbage through.

Sexual relations: When a person has ungodly sexual relations with another person, an ungodly soul tie is then formed (1 Corinthians 6:16, "What? Know ye not that he which is joined to a harlot is one body? For two, saith he, shall be one flesh."). This soul tie fragments the soul and is destructive. People who have many past relationships find it very difficult to 'bond' or be joined to anybody, because their soul is fragmented.

Being in the night life, he was always around women and mostly the type that didn't care if you had a girlfriend or not. He had temptation on every side and I know although he denied it, he fell prey to that temptation on multiple occasions. He wasn't what I needed, but I didn't want to let go. I was hanging on hoping that one day I would be enough for him. I wanted him to recognize that I loved him for who he was, not what he did. I hoped he would see that none of those other women would ever love him as I did. I wanted to spend my life making him happy, but in the end God knew best. When God says "No," trust that he has something/someone better for you. Don't get me wrong, he was a great person, he just wasn't the one for me. He knew that better than I did. God will do whatever is necessary to protect those that belong to him. In this case, he protected us both.

The day will eventually come when you look back and say "thank you Jesus for what you didn't allow me to have." Thank you for protecting me from disease and from an unwanted pregnancy. We parted ways for the last time when I relocated to Florida. He told me he should have married me a long time ago.

I didn't see it while we were dating, but at that moment, I realized that all his reasons for not marrying me or even living with me, was God's hand of protection. I never knew anything could be so painful. I cried for weeks on end, fighting the desire to pick up the phone and call him.

He was not dead, but I was a woman mourning over the loss of someone I had loved for what seemed like a lifetime. I wondered if I would ever be emotionally free from this man.

My only way out, the only thing I knew to do was fall on my face before the Lord and turn my thoughts away from what I perceived as a loss onto the one who is a Specialist at finding and redeeming the lost.

In this long term relationship, I was dealing with stuff no one knew about which was how I lived my life. I was miserable, tired and very lonely. I felt myself slowly being pulled into a very dark place and it began to manifest in my actions, health and physical appearance. Completely beaten emotionally, exhausted from trying to be all things to all people, and becoming increasingly disgusted with my appearance, I unknowingly gave Satan an open door. He took full advantage of it. He attacks when you are at your most vulnerable point.

During all this, my older sister Doris, (nicknamed cookie) was diagnosed with Breast Cancer. She died at the age of 34. I believe something changed in me as a result of her death. Of the six girls, she and I were the closest in age. I saw her as a troubled teenager and I watched in sadness as she struggled with drug addiction as an adult. I admired and looked up to her in spite of her lifestyle. Every chance I got, I tried to follow her wherever she went. I loved her so much. She was fairly rebellious as a teen and gave my mom hell. Like a wild horse that could not be tamed, she lived life dangerously and on edge. Why? I'm sure she found drugs and sex to be a coping mechanism. That was her escape from our reality and she never found her way to a peaceful existence. She would stay away from family whenever she was on a binge. The desire and pull of that lifestyle took her away from her beautiful baby girl and five other children that followed before her death. Years later when we found out she had breast cancer, she had six children. I didn't see her much after that.

I received a call one day that she was in the hospital. My sisters Amber and Patrice got there first, as I recall. I will never forget what they told me before they left. She asked them to fix her hair and clean her face. They had no idea that would be the last time they would see her. When I got there with my sister Carolyn and my brother Stevie, she was gone. Her body lay there cold and lifeless but she looked so peaceful. I was filled with despair at the thought that she died completely alone. I felt a deep sadness as I thought about the life she had. My brother's response to her laying in that bed was shocking. I had never seen him cry before. Oh my goodness, such deep and overwhelming grief hit me. Cookie was the first of the siblings to pass away and at the young age of thirty-four. She left behind six beautiful children; one that was only a year old. I grieved for my sister for more than two years it seemed, and that's when I believe all hell broke loose in my life. But one night, I had the most beautiful dream of Cookie which totally set me free… at least from the grief. This is the dream:

I was standing in a room full of family members and suddenly she appeared to me. I gasped because I couldn't believe I was seeing her but, I also couldn't understand why no one else was responding. They clearly didn't see her. She walked towards me then stopped in front of me, staring for a minute and then she put her arms around me. No words were ever spoken but at that moment I felt an overwhelming peace come upon me.

The dream was so real. I remembered what she was wearing and how she smelled. When I woke up, I knew it was over. I knew that was God's way of releasing me from the pain I was struggling with. I needed to know that she was okay and most importantly that she was with Him.

My past childhood experiences and the death of my sister Cookie, unleashed a spirit of fear in me that took me years to overcome. After that experience, I continued to have nightmares. Not every now and again, but almost every night. It was so bad at one point; I was terrified to go to sleep at night. I could only drift off if a light was on or if I kept the TV on all night. It didn't stop the spiritual torment but it at least allowed me to fall asleep.

When I wasn't having nightmares, I was seeing images and hearing voices. I thought I was going crazy and of course I said nothing to anyone. My brother and I were sitting on the porch one day; just talking and we got on the subject of dreams. He shared a dream with me and expressed how much it scared him. I think he was expecting me to be shocked, but I wasn't. What he described was what I lived every day. That was the first time I told anybody about my experience(s). He was shocked. On another occasion, while lying in the bed with my friend, he woke up startled and moved away from me. I asked him what was wrong with him. His response was, "did you not hear that growling sound you just made?" I hadn't heard anything but I did feel something and it wasn't of God.

Many times as I fell asleep, I would literally feel a weight on my back. It was like something just came down on my back. Sometimes it would sit on the side of my bed. I was aware of what was happening but I'd lay still, silently praying and resisting the impulse to open my eyes, afraid of what I would see. Many times, I felt like the life was being sucked out of me as I was unable to catch my breath. The moment I started praying, it would lift off. I learned years later that when the enemy is oppressing you, it could be an indication of what God has prepared for you. Whatever he has for me must be huge!

The amazing thing was that these events eventually led me to the Lord out of absolute fear. God knows what He's doing! As a child, I'd always felt drawn to REALLY know God. While going through all of this, I made the decision to go back to church. Witnessing the peace that my sister Lin had, I just knew I had to have it.

Then I had a dream one night that I was at the old house on School Street in the front yard. I saw Lin walking with a man that had no features, but I recall her looking so peaceful and happy and I said to myself, "I want that kind of peace."

I started going to her church and it opened up a whole new world for me. One Sunday during the altar call, I felt a burning heat rise up through me that caused me to leap out of my seat and run to that altar. What the enemy meant for my harm, God was about to turn around for my good. That represented a new beginning for me, but it did not stop the hell I was going through. However, I had just been given new weapons to fight with.

My decision to turn to the Lord was also creating a new issue in my already dysfunctional, long-term relationship. God was really dealing with me about fornicating. I really didn't want to do it anymore, but I also didn't want to lose him. Needless to say, I clung to my relationship with the Lord, but not in a way that was pleasing to him. Can you say compromise? That's what I was doing.

At the time, everything else in my life was going fairly well. I was working for a great company and enjoying the fruit of my labor. In the meantime, I found out my sister Amber was struggling with a drug addiction that often times pulled her away from her children. It was as if history was repeating itself like with Cookie. During this time, she and her children were living at home with mama. Although my mom loved having her granddaughters with her and did all she could to take care of them, she was not in a financial position to care for them and was getting too old to raise more kids. Amber ultimately made the choice to walk away. For her, it was better to leave than for her children and family members to witness the devastating effect the drugs took on her.

With no real plan or thought, I made the decision to take custody of my two beautiful nieces, Danielle and Adrienne. Danielle was living with my mom and at the time Adrienne lived with her dad. I knew my mom could not properly take care of Dani and I did not want them to be separated, so I spoke with Adrienne's dad about keeping them together. Being a single dad, he agreed to my plan. People applauded me for taking them in, but what people didn't know was that those two girls saved my life. They were my heart and my reason to succeed.

With the new responsibility of raising kids, I became much more focused and less concerned about pleasing myself. I was hell bent on giving them a good life and doing well in my job and God surely blessed me. I excelled and was promoted many times. I wanted to give them a stable, healthy and happy life, which was something I never had. They were the best kids. Well disciplined, respectful and never asked for anything.

To be able to give our children the life they deserve sometimes comes at a price and requires great sacrifice. With the latest promotion, my job required a greater commitment of my time. I began working excessively to keep up with the requirements of the position. Hence, I ended up sacrificing time with my babies and being available for their needs. I was working between twelve and sixteen hours daily and that didn't include bringing work home. This just added to an already overwhelming and stressful life. They were struggling with the emotional challenges of having yet another absent mother and I was failing at giving them security and attention. I began perpetuating the issues they were having with their mother.

I took them to counseling as things got harder. Their mom would drop in and out. They were elated every time she came back and devastated when she left. I loved her but, I was angry at the same time because of what I saw her doing to those children. No matter what she did or didn't do, they never stopped loving their mother and I refused to give up on her. We lived with the daily fear of someone telling us she had been killed or died from an overdose.

Then a life changing event took place that I thought would be the end of me. My brother Stevie died. When I received the call, I yelled out in horror and immediately blamed myself. I called my friend, who at this time was living with someone else, but we remained dysfunctionally connected (always holding on). I didn't want to be disrespectful to his girlfriend, but he was the only one that could have consoled me but not even he could calm me down; I was absolutely hysterical.

I can't recall a time when I needed him as much as I did that day. I was desperate for his love and to be in the comfort of his arms. I would have given anything for it. The call ended with him asking me where I would be. I thought for sure he would come to my rescue... he never did. I was beyond hurt and so disappointed that after years of being there for him, he chose not to be there for me. Stevie and Glenn had just been at my house the night before. They wanted to spend the night as they had planned to do some work for me the next day. Well, I was planning to have an overnight guest, so that wasn't going to work for me. I remember Stevie looking really sunburned, but he was in good spirits. They ate something and then went home.

The guilt I felt was overwhelming. If I had just let him stay this may not have happened. I thought that my decision to satisfy my flesh had just caused my brother's untimely death from a cocaine overdose. To add salt to the self- inflicted wound, after the funeral, my brother Glenn who was with Stevie that night, told me that it was my fault he was dead.

Clearly, he had the same thought that I had.

Mourning the death of my brother, the lack of sleep, the stress at work, and the constant battles at night caused my body to shut down. I gained weight and I was exhausted all the time. I got to a place where I too wanted to die. I would wake up in the night and sit on my bed in tears, asking God to please let me die. The tormenting spirit was so heavy at times, I would look in the mirror fully expecting to see something other than my own reflection starring back at me. I felt a constant presence of evil around me; especially during the night. I didn't know it then, but I had fallen into a deep state of depression.

Stevie and I were very close. I looked up to him and was always extremely proud of him. It's funny that my fondest memory of him was of him teaching me the art of grooming for a man (shaving and cutting hair) as he prepared to go out. Stevie was always meticulous about his appearance and always carried himself with dignity (until the alcohol and drugs took over). He was the first to make an attempt to teach me how to drive a standard shift car. I failed miserably and damaged his cute little blue Fiat convertible. He never spoke a harsh word and I never saw him raise his voice. He was a quiet and good hearted person, but he was clearly deeply wounded himself, to turn to drugs and alcohol the way that he did. His addiction was not as visible as it was with my other siblings.

I never thought he would get caught up in that lifestyle, but that's what repressed pain can do.

With all my heart, I believe that his life took a downward spiral when his first wife divorced him. He disconnected and lost his drive and passion for life. He turned to destructive things and people to fill the void. At the time of his death, I think his biggest regret was losing his ex-wife and his daughter. I don't think he ever stopped loving his first wife but he was too proud to admit it.

A few years later, another devastating blow came with the death of a longtime friend. It felt like I spent years overwhelmed with grief. After this loss, I found myself getting ready for work one morning around 5:30am with such heaviness in my heart. I was drenched with tears, not wanting to be in this life and dreading having to go through another stressful day at work. I pushed myself to get there, barely able to see thru my tears.

I sat at my desk for maybe fifteen minutes; tears flowing and all the life draining from me. I just couldn't think clearly or function. In deep distress, I called my dad (something I'd NEVER done before) asking him to help me. I literally broke down on the phone and I know that scared him. He asked me if I wanted him to call one of my sisters (Carolyn or Lin) to come pick me up. I was working in downtown DC at the time. I gathered my composure long enough to realize that there was no help to be had. I told him I'd be okay and hung up the phone. Within minutes, I picked up the phone and called my doctor - again something I never did. She gave me an appointment right away. "Amazing Grace, how sweet the sound that saved a wretch like me." Wow… that just calmed my spirit because I see that phone call was God's hand ordering my steps.

With seemingly all the weight of the world on my shoulders, I picked up my bags and walked right out of my office. I don't think I even called anybody to tell them I was leaving. I got to work so early, no one else was in. The first question the doctor asked me was "are you feeling suicidal?" I told her that had been on my mind constantly, but I knew I would never do it because of my understanding at the time, of the spiritual implications behind such an act. I desperately wanted to make sure that I would see my loved one's again after death. She felt I should check-in to a facility if I still had those feelings, but I told her I didn't think that would be necessary. I just wanted relief. I wanted to be able to sleep through the night. I wanted my pain to go away. That was the start of my almost two-year struggle with clinical depression. I couldn't go back to work. I was put on short-term disability, which ended up turning into long-term disability.

After the medical diagnosis of depression, I began treatment with a psychiatrist which was accompanied by drugs that put me in a zombie state of mind. I would literally sit around all day starring into space or I'd just sleep. My help came when I was led to a mental health counselor. Get this… the name of the facility was Agape Mental Health, meaning: selfless; sacrificial and unconditional love. God is always in control.

I wasn't thrilled about going, fearing what might be discovered if someone was able to break through the walls I had built around myself. I didn't know what to expect, but this lady pulled stuff out of me that I didn't know was there. For the first time, I had to dig deep, take a look at myself (the hardest thing to do), confront my issues and let go of what she called "My Savior Complex." My problem was that I had a need to fix everybody. I spent years taking on the burdens and weight of others, which God never intended for me to carry. I had become an enabler to many. I took more of an interest in everybody else, but didn't take care of myself very well. That was really a shocker when she put a label on what I was doing. I learned later that putting yourself first was not being selfish. If you don't take care of self, you can't take care of anyone else. Thank God for these life lessons. I still struggle with taking care of myself, but I am getting better.

During one of my sessions, I remember being so weak from crying as she pushed me to dig deeper into my inner self. She looked at me and actually said, "I'm afraid you may not make it through another crisis." That's how I felt too. Be careful what you speak; your words have life. Not long after she spoke those words, yet another devastating death in my family. This time, it was my oldest brother who we lovingly nicknamed "Fuzzy." That caused a major setback in my therapy.

Fuzzy was a character but like Stevie, everybody loved him and like Stevie, he medicated himself with drugs and alcohol. He had been sober for a couple of years before his death. However, many years of heavy drug and alcohol use caught up with him. Because he had been doing so well, no one was expecting this and it happened so quickly. He was gone by the time his children reached him in the hospital. Still slightly "off" myself, thanks to the medication, I went into the room where his body was laying and I stared and cried so hard that I actually thought I saw him move. I grabbed him and just held him asking God to bring him back as if loving him would be enough. I was so out of it, I contemplated getting on the gurney with him, but someone came in...thank God. They probably would have sent me to the nut house and I wouldn't have blamed them.

I was beginning to feel like I was never going to get better. I feared that I would never again have a normal, peaceful life. I tried to go back to work and I didn't last one day. I was on so many anti-depressants and sleep aids that I didn't know what world I was in most of the time. My family, God bless them, took over caring for Danielle and Adrienne because I was in no position to do so other than financially. They watched over them and me, which included keeping me protected from myself.

After about a year, I finally started to come around. I was grateful for the opportunity to just be at home and rest. It was GREAT being able to sleep through the night with no encounters to rob me of my peace. After many years of being distant, I started spending a lot of time with my dad in those days, which I enjoyed so much. We developed a relationship I wish I'd had with him as a child. He would come down and visit with me and my mom. That was really amazing. We would take drives together visiting family just like old times. The only difference, they were happy to be together and we laughed and enjoyed each other's company. They had been separated for years by this time, so mama was living with my sister Patrice and her husband.

While picking up one of the kids from school one day, I noticed this cute little house right across the street with a "for sale" sign. It sat on a huge piece of property with the most beautiful green grass and a long front porch. My mind started clicking and I got a notion to show it to my dad. He was still living at our family home with a few of my older brothers.

I was so excited on his next visit, I asked him to come take a look at it with me. Never in a million years did I think it would be something that he would entertain. When we walked in, we were greeted by a beautiful black Grand piano which was placed next to a brick fireplace. My immediate thought was, "this is home." I tried to contain my excitement, but as we looked around, I began to paint a picture of what my dream home/family could have been in a home like this as a child. I could tell he was getting excited the more I spoke of this home, as though it was already his. I talked about the family gatherings we could have around that fireplace; listening to him play the piano as we all sang along. We spoke of having family gatherings in the backyard, playing softball and horse shoes, etc. We made plans for how the basement could be turned into another living area to include bedrooms.

He was sold on the idea. Of course that meant getting my mom to be in agreement to come back home. At this time, he had sold one piece of property and was working on a deal to sell the home place, so he had some cash on hand and felt sure he could obtain a loan for the remainder. I told daddy that I was willing to sell my house to ensure the funds would be available to purchase this property but he would not agree to that. We had it all planned out. There would be space for me and the girls. So, we did a walk through with mama and others in the family. Everybody loved it. My dad took the next steps to acquire the property, but to no avail.

Ultimately I believe that was just a means God used to bring my parents back into relationship. Daddy spent a lot of time with mama after that. It was approaching the date of their anniversary, since they never legally divorced. During one of our visits, I asked him about doing something special for mama. He gave me a big smile and wanted to know what I had in mind. I knew she had never had a wedding ring so I suggested he purchase one for her. Off we went to the jeweler and to my surprise he purchased a beautiful diamond wedding ring with no concern about the cost. For me, that made up for all the years of sadness and disappointment in him as a child. I was so proud of him and so full of love.

The next step was planning the actual anniversary celebration. We made plans for the gathering to be at my home. Everyone was excited and willing to fully participate in the festivities, including the nieces, nephews and grandkids. Only a couple of people knew about the ring. After we had eaten our fill, we gathered in the dining room and sat mama and daddy down in chairs to present them their gifts. Finally, it was time for him to present. I was on pins and needles. He turned to my mom and simply said, "something I should have given you years ago... I love you."

Gasps, screams and tears were the responses of everyone in the room. There was not a dry eye in the house and mama was beyond shocked. As if I was standing on the outside looking in, I observed all the responses and was utterly shocked by the tears I saw well up in my brothers' eyes. They had never seen my dad express love towards my mom and something in each of them seemed to change. I saw years of anger and disappointment melt away. The icing on the cake was when my dad looked at us and said OUT LOUD... "I love all my kids." Jesus, what a healing moment that was! I immediately felt a sense of sadness, but I couldn't understand why. The answer to my "why" eventually was made painfully clear.

Only a few months later, on a cold, winter evening, I received a call that daddy had been rushed to the hospital. At that moment, instead of reverting back into the darkness of depression, an inner strength rose up in me. I woke up with a new level of determination in my spirit, "I was not going to live through yet another tragedy by taking pills." I knew if I didn't stop then, I too could become dependent on substances to get thru the day. So, I made the abrupt decision to stop cold turkey, despite the warning I received by the psychiatrist. I felt like my test was in being able to deal with the pain of this latest crisis by being fully present and aware.

When I arrived at the emergency room, daddy was awake and alert, but very weak. He was having challenges breathing. We assumed this happened because of the strong smell of Kerosene fumes in his home when my nephew found him.

When they took him to his room, he seemed stronger and was talking and laughing with the Doctor. Instead of focusing on the issue of his breathing, he was asking the doctor about the challenges he was having with walking. I was standing beside him when they came in to give him a breathing treatment. Within minutes after that breathing treatment, he was gasping for air. He looked at me with absolute fear, reached for me to come closer and asked me to fan him. I was terrified as it seemed daddy was having a heart attack right in front of me. The nurses were there immediately and connected him up to IV's and a breathing machine. They eventually took him away to have a stint placed in his heart. When they brought him back he was in a medically induced coma. How had the situation turned so badly, so quickly?

The next day I went to visit. It was just he and I, so I took the opportunity to talk to him privately. I felt as though he would hear me even if he wasn't able to respond. I held his hand in mine and spoke these words in his ear, "I forgive you daddy." Then I told him how much we all loved him and thanked him for being the best father he knew how to be to his children. He squeezed my hand and when I looked up I saw tears coming from his eyes. I knew then that he heard me.

I don't even remember how many days went by before they called the family to gather for their final goodbyes. They attempted to bring him out of the coma several times, but each time it caused more stress on his heart. The doctor told us that they could bring him out, but it would cause him a great deal of pain, but there was nothing more they could do for him. So, here we are gathered around my father's bedside and they tell my mom she needs to make the decision to remove him from life support. I cringed at the thought and was disturbed at the decision, but ultimately realized it was necessary. The nurse prepared us for what would take place during the process of disconnecting the machine. As we all stood by quietly, Lin read a scripture and sang a hymn.

True to my character, I felt the need to show strength in front of my family. I didn't want them to think I was going to have another melt down. So I stood at his bedside along with my family and dared myself to shed a tear. I was demonstrating strength under pressure, so I thought. That ended up being absolute foolishness. You must allow yourself to express emotions; that's why God gave them to you. If you hold it in for so long, like a volcano, one day out of the blue there will be a major eruption. I said to myself, "I refuse to allow myself to grieve" - bad idea. I watched my dad draw his last breath, with tears in his eyes, but surrounded by all of his children.

I know that silent healing was happening within him during his transition and God was preparing him for his journey home. I believe that the tears came because he knew we were all there and that finally, all had been forgiven. What a way to enter eternity.

CHAPTER 4
Deliverance
Joy Comes in the Morning

"… and God shall wipe away every tear from their eyes." (Rev 21:4)

Oddly enough, suffering silently over my dad's death was my turnaround. The devil tried to destroy me, but God had a plan to restore me.

I was still on disability. The girls, still lived with me, but were being taken care of by the village (my siblings). Even though I abruptly took myself off all medications, I was coping well at home without them. I was starting to mentally become more focused and began to piece together the fragments of my broken life.

One day I was at my desk typing and singing along with my worship music. Suddenly, I literally felt something heavy lift off of me. I knew it was God. In that instant, He delivered me from evil and restored my peace. I was so full of joy and excitement. I started praising God right where I was. Being so overwhelmed, I ran out of my house and made a bee line to my sister's house (well it was only up the sidewalk) to share what had just happened with her. We both started laughing and thanking God. I couldn't even remember the last time I had smiled. You just could not imagine the joy and peace I felt in just one moment. Weeping endured for a long night, but joy did come in the morning.

Never underestimate the power of true, heartfelt worship to God. It can break every chain that binds you. I have always had a love for music - I love to sing. Nothing moves me more than listening to worship music. Secular music was on my playlist, but there was something about connecting to God with nothing holding me back… just me and Him.

I felt a sense of joy for my family as well. I knew and I could see the despair and sadness in their hearts as they watched me disappear into my own little world of silence. I knew it was as much a relief for them as it was for me. I say again, "thank God for family." While I was going through this nightmarish hell, they were right there. We often laugh and joke about what they saw during that time - I was so out of it. I couldn't recall some of the things they said I did. It was sad, but none the less very true.

When that depressive spirit was broken off my life I had a peace that I'd never experienced before. For the first time in years, I was able to lay my head down and I slept like a baby with no disturbances, no visitations or dreams; just a sweet sleep in Jesus. Realizing the next morning that I'd slept through the night, I had a smile on my face that could have penetrated any darkness that remained. Thank God, there was no darkness, only the light of His love shining in me and all around me. I was under a halo of his warmth, love and protection. "With long life you will satisfy me, my Lord and my Savior."

As I think back to my treatment for depression, one thing absolutely puzzled me. I couldn't understand why in the world they would treat people for depression/suicidal thoughts with drugs that cause you to be depressed, moody and suicidal.

In all of this, I caution you... depression is real. As with incest and molestation, it is an ugly spirit that can take hold of you without you even knowing it. If life ever becomes overwhelming, or you become disinterested in the things that you use to enjoy, or if you feel yourself wanting to be alone more than usual, please talk to someone. The silence can be deadly.

There is no doubt that God can heal you instantly but in the meantime, exercise wisdom in deciding on the course of treatment that best fits your needs while you wait on God for your healing and deliverance. He can and He will. He is no respecter of persons. He did it for me and countless others, He can and will do it for you. I speak the truth when I tell you, it only takes a moment of isolation (the enemy's tactic) and a spirit of heaviness to push you into making a decision that will take you away from people that love and care about you. Don't let the enemy take your life; it doesn't belong to him. Get help and seek Godly counsel. There is a balm in Gilead to heal your soul.

CHAPTER 5
The Exodus
Florida Bound

Not long after my father passed, my sister Lin and niece Erica asked me to consider moving to Florida. What????? Normally, I could not have imagined leaving my family or Virginia. Until Lin and Erica moved, our entire family lived in Virginia. But God's timing is always perfect. He had created the perfect opportunity and cleared the way for me to consider doing a new thing; pushing me out of my comfort zone and the comfortable little nest I created for myself.

At that point, I was no longer on official disability. My entire department had been given the option to move to Chicago and or be laid off. "I quickly replied, I'll take lay-off for $1,000 Alex!" ...a little humor there.

I thought there was no way I would abandon my family; especially if it meant taking the girls away from everything and everyone that was familiar to them after just losing my siblings, my dad and my friend. I had no fear of being laid off. I received a severance package and I knew I had enough experience to get another job somewhere. The economy in 2004 was nothing like it is now, thank you Jesus.

I contemplated the decision. As much as I could not

imagine leaving my family, the thought of starting over again in sunny Florida, (a place I always considered a resort destination) was creating an excitement in me. Once I prayed about it and felt a peace in my spirit, I called them and told them I had made the decision to come and would be looking into preparations to sell my house. As God would have it, I just happened to live next door to a realtor. While doing my lawn one day, I asked him about listing my house.

He came in, did a quick tour of all three levels and explained the process, fee etc. He was willing to take less on commission just to help me out. "That sounds good," I thought... well, it got even better, but oh so scary. He called the next day and asked if he could bring a family by. "Sure, no problem" I responded. I didn't have to do any major cleaning because my house was always clean (great child rearing by my mom who was a neat freak). The same day, they made an offer which made me almost pass out. My God is greater, my God is stronger, and God you are higher than any another. My house sold for three times what I paid for it. No turning back at this point. We had to move and they wanted to move in right away. "What you say!"

So, the girls and I began preparing physically and emotionally for our departure. I still couldn't believe I was doing this. During the time of my depression, Amber was in and out of the girls' lives, but before we moved, after so many years being out in the street and struggling with her addiction, God brought her home and gave her a chance at a new beginning. One day out of the blue, I received a call from my mom and my two youngest sisters Amber and Beth. I heard, "Hey guess what? We're coming to Florida too." It couldn't have worked out more perfectly. The girls would be reunited with their mom, in addition to the sister already in Florida. That meant I would have three of my sisters, my mom and the girls with me.

It felt like the Beverly Hillbillies as we loaded up the truck. It turned out to be THE saddest exodus ever!!!! For the rest of the family, we would only be a few hours away by plane, but you would have thought we were never going to see each other again. Our neighbors and family that remained on School Street planned a going away gathering for mama that we all enjoyed. It was her final goodbye to all the people we grew up with. It was just like old times... Everyone gathered around dancing, talking and just enjoying the time together.

We had a final family picnic at Patrice's house, then the kids and I were off to the airport. I think I cried the entire way to Florida and I knew the kids probably did as well. We were greeted with open arms by Lin and Erica. Our lives were about to change drastically, but for the better.

All I can say is... NEVER say never! You don't know the strength you have until you take that scary leap of faith into unchartered territory; the times when God stretches you beyond your human capacity. I'm so glad He did. The Lord truly ordered my steps. Thanks to the huge profit I made from the house, the girls and I were financially secure and I didn't have to rush to find employment. My sisters, Beth and Amber were due to arrive in a couple of weeks, with mama.

The next thing on the family agenda was trying to find the right house for mama and the girls. My niece Erica took charge of this process (which she loved) and drove us around to several new home developments. She had such a gift for this type of thing and was an excellent negotiator. It didn't take long before she found the perfect neighborhood. Now, let me tell you how much of a sense of humor God has. The neighborhood that mama chose to move into was built by "Smith Family Homes." When we saw that driving into the development, we all laughed and knew this was going to be the new family home. For a short time (a month or so) we all stayed at Lin's four-bedroom house until my mom's house was built. For some families, that may have been overwhelming, but not for mine. We loved being together and were certainly accustomed to being squeezed together like sardines. We always made the best of such situations.

After living in poverty all of our lives and for my mom everything in life having been a struggle, her prayers were finally answered. Her "ship" had finally come in. Ironically, the financial blessing for us all came as a result of my father's death. There was a nice settlement from the sale of the family property on School Street, but my dad initially was hell bent on not giving a penny to my mom. In the end, she got her portion and his which ultimately allowed her to buy her home, which she had always intended to be a place for all of her children. And so it is and if my prayers are answered, the debt will be cancelled and it will remain an inheritance for my siblings.

The memories we made in this home will never be forgotten. It has been a resting place, a safe haven and a place where Love lives and the family has thrived. That's all she ever said she wanted… to be loved. Thanks mama for your years of unselfish love.

When I made the decision to come to Florida, not only was it a realization of having to start over in an unfamiliar place, but it also required a leap of faith to embrace the need to enlarge my territory. Would I be able to move forward? Would I be able to be set free from a long term relationship? More than anything I wanted to be free; I wanted a new beginning… a fresh start.

I was determined that I was not going to bring into my new life, the weight and baggage of my past. It was time to completely let go; like Paul, I had to leave those things behind and press on towards the mark of the high calling of Jesus Christ.

My sick, dysfunctional cycles of life had to be buried with my past. It was time for my "dry bones" to live. I survived leaving my long-term lover behind and I had to forgive and release family members for the detestable things done to me. Once all of that had been dealt with, I was on a mission to find God for myself.

After everyone got settled in their new homes, it was just me and Lin. Since I hadn't yet found a job, I used my time to draw close to God in a fresh, new way. I had a hunger and thirst to know God like never before. I was completely fixated on anything that would allow God to reveal himself to me. I would sit for hours on end watching Christian Broadcasting stations – feasting on God's word and receiving fresh revelation.

During this time, since this was the first time a group of us had separated from the home place, we instituted what we lovingly called our weekly "family conference calls." In this way, those of us in Florida, could reach out and keep in touch with the family in Virginia. It initially started with just the girls. For the first time ever, we found ourselves talking and sharing with one another about our past. That opened the door and was the start of breaking the cycle of that Generational Curse I mentioned earlier. Now we actually had a dialogue amongst us girls and the healing had begun.

Remember the family letter that I spoke of earlier? Well, as we started to discuss the letter on our conference calls, other family members began to share their experiences. If you recall, in my mind for many years, I assumed I had been the only one. However, my sister Beth decided to confront my mom about what happened to her.

We were all overwhelmed with emotion as the truth was unveiled. Each of us had a story. My sister, Lin was just crushed at the thought of us (the younger girls) having gone through such an ordeal. As we talked about it, she sat on the couch in tears. I'm sure the source of her tears was a feeling of personal guilt and shame (although not warranted) that she wasn't there to protect us or her own daughter – that she didn't know until then was also a victim.

Eventually, the conference calls included the entire family. That was probably no coincidence either. We came to look forward to those early Saturday morning phone calls. There was always laughter. Even though words had not been spoken, there was healing and forgiveness taking place....to some degree anyway. For that, I was grateful and for me, life was good. I had dealt with the enemies of my past and I was ready for my new journey to begin. In exposing this truth about my family, I pray that for those that read this book they will have a sense to repent and ask for God's forgiveness, forgive themselves so they can be set free from that dark cloud of guilt and shame that often occurs with this spirit of perversion.

For those that are having a challenge in the area of forgiveness, I share this message with you from a Facebook Post by Iyanla Vanzant:

Forgiveness is a process of giving up the old for something new. Old experiences and memories that we hold on to in anger, resentment, shame, or guilt cloud our spirit mind. The truth is everything that has happened had to happen. It was a growth experience. There was something you needed to know or learn. If you stay angry, hurt, afraid, ashamed, or guilty, you miss the lesson. You will be stuck in a cloud of pain.

In order to walk in forgiveness, I shared this letter with my family.

Dear Family,

I made a conscious decision not to remain in that place of pain, shame or fear. So for those who harmed me physically and emotionally, I tell you, I love each of you with all my heart and no act, no transgression, no inappropriate thought or desire will ever cause me to love you any less. My desire is that you experience the best life God has for you.

As I write these words, the story of Moses comes to mind. This really was an "exodus" both in the natural and in the spirit for my entire family. God was delivering us from what was and now is bringing us into our promised land. A whole new life was awaiting us and Lin was the catalyst that God used to bring it all together.

Through my sister, Amber's many years of struggles with drug addiction and now understanding how that was directly connected to the abuse that she endured, I found myself, often trying to save her from the streets, while maintaining complete confidence that one-day God would deliver her. Because of that, no matter how many times she ran away, I never gave up on her and it was well worth it. For example, I recall a visit to Virginia at Christmas in 2004. It was shortly after they joined us and moved to Florida.

Amber drove the girls and my mom back to Virginia to celebrate Christmas with the rest of the family. At this time, she was doing very well and was completely drug free. So much so, that I wasn't at all concerned about her returning home, so close to her old stomping grounds in Washington, DC. My sister, Patrice opened her home in Maryland to all of us for the holidays, and we were having a great time together, like old times. Then temptation struck and the opportunity presented itself. Amber was given some money and the next thing we knew, she said she was going to the store and would be back shortly. She didn't come back.

The next day after realizing what likely happened, I was furious with her for inflicting such pain on all of us, but especially for her two daughters, whose mother has now gone missing right before Christmas. My other sisters and I gathered to talk, trying to figure out what to do, since she had not only left but she left with our mother's car. In the environment we knew she would be in, we were afraid the car may be stolen and/or sold. As we started to fear the worst, we came to the conclusion that we had to find her. Now, I knew my younger sisters were on board with this idea, but I never expected my older sister to be willing to go into unknown parts of a very dangerous part of the city to look for her. Our brothers cautioned us in what we were about to do, but not one of them offered to go with us.

Anyway, we jumped in my sister's car, not having a clue where to look, but I can only believe that Holy Angels were guiding us all the way. I drove into an area of South East, Washington, D.C., which I had driven through on many occasions, trying to find her in the past. We drove and drove. We turned up one street and down the next, looking for my mother's car. Finally, I turned into one particular neighborhood, (completely directed of the Holy Spirit) and there on the corner, was my mother's car. God had ordering our footsteps and protected us, as well. We were so excited about finding the car, that our first response was to get the car and run the opposite direction, as quickly as possible. We stood out on the sidewalk for a minute, wondering if we should take a risk by knocking on apartment doors asking about her, but we quickly came to our senses and realized that, that was THE dumbest idea and completely unsafe.

After standing on the sidewalk for a few minutes, unsure on what to do next, we saw Amber walking down the sidewalk with some guy. Talk about God meeting us where we're at? She appeared to be sober, and was shocked to see us standing there. I am sad to say that my first reaction was of outright anger. I boldly approached her and spewed out language that was uncharacteristic of myself, but clearly reflected my thoughts of her in that moment. She was hurt, embarrassed and she apologized, but I turned and walked away. Then, suddenly the Holy Spirit spoke to me, "What are you doing? Didn't you come here to get her? Don't leave her on these streets!" By this time, my sister called her husband for help. Within minutes, he came barreling down the road in his truck, and after a few minutes of arguing with Amber (because she didn't want to come back), we literally picked her up and threw her into my brother-in-law's truck and he pulled away, leaving me and my sister on the street corner, wondering how in the heck we were going to find our way out of there. Needless to say, we managed, thanks to the Guardian Angels that covered us along the way. That was the last incident that Amber had with the drug life in Washington, D.C. She has been clean and sober ever since. To God be the Glory for this story of rescue and redemption!

After seeing for myself, how God can turn around any situation, I will never give up on those that I love, who also struggle with addiction. As long as there is breathe in their bodies, God can do the impossible, because God is love and love NEVER fails!

CHAPTER 6
Spiritual Awakening
Knowing God

Being new to Florida, and having not secured a job yet or put myself in a position to make any friends, (which wasn't easy for me) I spent a lot of time at home alone while Lin was at work. I had developed a great routine. Since Lin and I were dieting, I would prepare breakfast and lunch for her to take to work (to keep her from eating out). That could appear to be an unusual thing to do for a grown woman, but Lin meant the world to me. She was as kind and generous as she was beautiful, so it was my pleasure to do anything I could for her (more about her later).

Once the house was in order, I sat with my note pad and watch Christian TV. I was raised in a Baptist Church and before moving to Florida, I had given my life to the Lord but never really had a relationship with Him. I guess you can say I knew of God, but had no relationship with Him. My favorite television ministries were TD Jakes, Jamal Bryant, Bill Winston and Joyce Meyer. I could sit and soak all day; I was so intrigued by the teachings. As my spirit was fed daily, I realized that up until then, I wasn't actually learning, I was being preached at. I would sometimes sit in the living room with my Bible and become overwhelmed with emotions, as I took in every word.

The tears flowed until I had no more tears to cry. The more I read, listened and watched, the more I wanted to know. Most importantly, I wanted to know who this "Holy Spirit" was they kept talking about. I knew about Jesus, Angels and God, but I had never heard about the Holy Spirit. So now I was in hot pursuit to find out more. My niece, Erica told me about this church in Tampa her husband had been attending. So without any thought, we made plans to attend. It was the largest church I had ever attended. I was in awe walking into it. I was warmly embraced and welcomed by the ushers and greeters. The sound coming from the sanctuary was just amazing and energizing. As I looked around I was surprised to see that the congregation was filled with people of all nationalities and seemingly excited to be there. To my utter amazement and shock, the pastor came out to give his sermon and as he began to speak, I noticed he was Caucasian. I thought I would fall out! In my mind I said to myself, "Lord this has to be you." His message was talking about leaving people behind. Well, he certainly had my attention and from there, I knew I was "home." The Lord sent me to the place I needed to be so I could be refreshed, restored and fed. I didn't know it at the time, but all the answers to the deep questions I had about God all my life were about to be answered. I was about to meet God and experience his presence in a powerful way.

Only after a few short months, I was on fire for God. I went to service every time the doors opened. I started meeting some great women and God started mending my brokenness. This felt really good, but the more I grew the more I felt the need to get involved. So, since I was only working part-time at this point, I decided to volunteer a couple of days a week for the ministry. The receptionist introduced me to a young lady named Emily. She and I connected instantly. I helped her with administrative tasks, phone calls and errands as needed.

Then one day, as things were slow for her, she introduced me to a lady named Diana Lynn Gaddey - a divine connection. What started out for me as an instruction from her to assist in making follow up phone calls to visitors, became the starting point to my spiritual awakening. It was a journey that I could not have dreamed up in my wildest imagination.

I looked forward to seeing her. She had a way of making you feel comfortable, welcomed and loved. I watched her interact with other ladies who seemed to have a great love and affection for her as well. It didn't take long for me to see that she was an untapped resource in this ministry. Her title was Ladies Ministry Pastor, but she more than fulfilled this role with poise, grace and a humble spirit. Can you tell how much I love her yet? She became a voice of wisdom to me. My assignment with her directly was short lived, but God stretched me and pulled me out of my comfort zone. The thing I had feared the most, praying for others, God slammed me right into. As is always the case, He was preparing me for what was to come. My season was about to change and Pastor Diana Lynn was proof that God has people assigned to each level of your journey to guide you into your destiny. Hence the reason that it is critical that you follow His leading because someone else's life is dependent upon your obedience.

My heart for God, faithfulness and commitment to serve paid off with a great opportunity. It was if God created a position just for me. I was offered an administrative position with the ministry. I couldn't believe how fortunate I was to be given this opportunity. I embraced it whole heartedly, because in my perception, I was working directly for "God" and not for man. During one of the many times of ministry, I was told that I was there to learn what to do and what not to do. I am confident that mission was completed.

I met and worked with some wonderful people. I had the opportunity to travel on a regular basis and regularly saw God appear and move in supernatural ways. To say that I found out who God was would be an understatement. I was encountering God consistently and those encounters shifted the course of my life by preparing me for my destiny. What a ride it was and continues to be.

God wants to heal us in every place that we hurt. If you allow him to, the Holy Spirit will guide you out of every pit of life and change those obstacles into opportunities for ministry. Absolutely nothing is too hard for God and no trial, difficulty or adversity can stop the plan of God for your life unless you quit and give up. I say, "hold on, be strong, it's only a test." I look back and say, "What the enemy meant to harm me, God used for my good." I never could have made it without Him.

As much as I feasted on the word and basked in God's glory in Praise & Worship, no experience was more powerful to me than the Wednesday night bible study with Pastor Diana Lynn.

I felt connected to her the moment I met her, but I had no idea God would use this woman to open my world in ways I could never have fathomed.

She flowed in the gift of prophecy. At the time, I knew less about spiritual gifts than I did about the one who gave them; the Holy Spirit. I can't recall many gatherings where she did not minister in her gift. Initially, I came and just sat and listened quietly. I didn't understand what I was seeing or hearing but I knew I wanted **IT**.

She introduced me to the spiritual concept of birthing, foot washing, speaking in tongues, interpreting and what they deemed as "spiritual car wash." We would be so engulfed in a tangible move of God that we would be there for hours, long after the building had closed. When the presence of God is in the house, no one wants to go home.

This was a teaching ground for all of us ladies. As she came to know each of us, she started placing us in various areas to serve, as a means for our gifts to be brought forward and cultivated in what we knew was a very safe and loving environment. She continues to do that today, but just in a different venue.

On one occasion, she told us she was going to have each of us teach a lesson. She hadn't even called me yet and I was so nervous just anticipating having to stand up and speak in front of people. One night, she announced who was going to go first. After she called out the names, thinking I was safe this round, she said "Freda, God says your next." Oddly enough, I knew it before she even spoke it. That discernment was kicking in.

She had us do exercises to get comfortable hearing the sound of our own voice by speaking into the microphone. Who would think that such a simple task would be so uncomfortable, but she proved to be right. Once you get used to hearing your own voice, you become less apprehensive.

At this time, I had not experienced the Baptism of the Holy Spirit, nor had I ever been slain in the spirit. She had a young lady from the leadership team pray over me to receive it. Many others were brought up as well. I think I was the only one that night that didn't receive it immediately. Of course that left me thinking, "what is wrong with me?" As if sensing my disappointment, she said by the spirit of God, "some of you may not get it now, but by 12:00 midnight the Holy Spirit will come upon you." So, I went home completely expecting that something was going to happen.

Now hold onto your seats. That night I had an experience that I will never forget. In the middle of the night, I was awakened by a light hovering over me and the feeling of my head being lifted up from my neck off my pillow. I started speaking in what sounded to me like gibberish. It happened so quickly and all I can remember thinking is, "whatever this is, please don't stop."

I instinctively remembered what Pastor Diana Lynn had spoken and realized what was happening. So, I just laid still and let God do what He wanted to do. It was amazing. I had the presence of mind to look at the clock; it was 12:00 midnight. Look at God... right on time!

You cannot experience something like that and not be changed. I had many other visions and dreams after that night, which were equally unforgettable. For some reason, dreams and visions is the way God most often communicates with me. I'd have to say, it's no doubt because when I'm awake, I analyze everything. My mind is always flooded with various thoughts which I believe blocks me from hearing and receiving. So for me, how and who God uses to speak to me is not of great concern, I just want Him to keep on talking.

Freda N. Smith

CHAPTER 7
The Counterfeit
Pay Attention to the "Red Flags"

For the first time in my life, I was in such a good place. I was happy and living very comfortably. After volunteering and working a part-time job, I received a great job working for the ministry I previously volunteered for. My life was completely centered on Christ and that was working for me. Years prior to this period, I had a dream that I saw my sister Lin walking with a man. She seemed totally at peace. I could not see his face only the backside. In this dream, I said to myself, "I want whatever she has," which she confirmed one day when she shared, "I am satisfied with Jesus alone." With the life I was now living, it made perfect sense and I was beginning to understand what she meant. I can say in all truth that I was completely fulfilled in every area of my life, but...

The enemy comes to steal, kill and destroy!

Just when you think all is well because you're safe, happy and fulfilled the enemy of your soul (Satan) steps in to turn things upside down. What do I mean by this? Shortly after I began working for the ministry, I was introduced to a new employee by one of my co-workers. He appeared to be respectful, polite, intelligent, and had a heart for God. When I was introduced to him, he was working in the same office of the young lady I started volunteering for.

I was not at all looking to be in a relationship with anyone. I was not particularly drawn to him. Don't get me wrong, I surely had times when I felt lonely and would have enjoyed having someone to share my life with, but again I wasn't looking for anything. I was completely shocked when he expressed his desire to get to know me. I felt really stupid that I hadn't caught the hint, but at that time, I still had some major self-esteem issues. I remember asking myself, "why me?" There was so many beautiful women in that ministry.

We started talking and getting to know one another. I was surprised to find out from him, that he had been watching me for a while and finally got the nerve to approach me after attending a church event. Talking to him was very comfortable and he had a knack for making me laugh. That laugh... to this day, I will never forget how his laugh always brought a sense of longing, love, comfort and even a sense of safety to me. In the beginning, he never spoke an unkind word and always made me feel like I was the most important person in the room. I must say, after not thinking about being with a man, I quickly felt drawn to him and things began to move really fast; almost too fast for me. I wish I could say I proceeded with caution but, I did not. I was falling quickly and enjoying all the feelings that came along with it.

Only weeks after we began talking, he told me that

God told him I was going to be his wife. Now I thought that was really crazy, but something in me trusted everything that he said. I thought to myself, "you don't even know me". Little did I know, that statement was about to change my entire life and circumvent my confidence in relying on my ability to hear the voice of the Holy Spirit for myself.

As a result of his conversation and his actions, I had no reason to doubt the sincerity of his statement. I trusted the Holy Spirit in him completely and I was naive in thinking that, because he was an ordained Pastor that he was trustworthy. I soon learned that having a "title" has nothing to do with your character or personality traits. The issue soon caused me to get lost in him and not listen to that still small voice in my own spirit that was talking to me. I got so caught up in my emotions and the hype of feeling like God had answered my prayers in this man, I lost sight of everything. I was head over heels in love…. or was it lust? I wish I knew then what I have come to know now. I had been taken in by what I honestly believe was a seductive spirit which had slithered in through the cracks of what I thought was a strong armor. The **seductive spirit** in me was joined by a **counterfeit spirit** operating in him. Does that mean either of us were bad people? Absolutely not. The enemy will catch you when you are most vulnerable and use your weaknesses against you. At this stage, we both had cracks in our armor which Satan used to distract me from my relationship with God and him, from receiving the emotional healing God wanted to do in his life.

I was visiting him at his apartment one night and he became very angry as I was preparing to go home. He didn't want me to leave because he hated being alone (alone with his thoughts I believe). I went home anyway, but not long after being there, he called me and demanded that I come back. Well, as weird as that may sound, I took that as a sign of strength and his desire to be with me. So without any hesitation, I got back in my car and went to him and stayed overnight. This was my introduction to the **controlling spirit**. As you can see from my experiences, no matter how many signs God throws up, your flesh will pull you in the direction it wants to go and my flesh was on fire!

Within months, we were inseparable! I loved being with him and he with me, or so they thought. We both became church fanatics, very seldom missing any event that took place. It was work, church and home for us both. In less than a year of us getting together, he proposed to me while having lunch in a restaurant. I said yes, even though I felt resistance within. Things were moving too fast, but I didn't want to lose what I thought was my blessing from God. As each moment of doubt arose, those words filled my head, "God said you are my wife!!" Not long after he proposed, he convinced me to move in with him. After all we were going to be married, right? The **spirit of manipulation** was in full effect. I was disappointed in myself when I notified Lin about my decision. She never judged me for a decision we both knew was wrong, and she strongly encouraged me not to do it. I know I hurt her that day and I will forever regret that decision.

Once again, I knew better, but I didn't act on what I knew. So now, we are living together without being married, sleeping in the same bed and convincing ourselves that there was no harm in that. When you want what you want, you will convince yourself that it's okay. We were both still working for the ministry, but things were becoming very strained for us because I knew I was living a lie.

However, my family was so excited and happy that I found someone. At the first meeting, they fell in love with him. My mother was really impressed by him and enjoyed his company. He was a gifted communicator among other things. Since so much of my life centered on the church, we both spent a great deal of time working, attending and serving. I thought it was rather special that he even wanted to attend the ladies Bible study with me each week. We were always together. The more time we spent together, it was clear he was very anxious to be married, more so than I was even though he had just ended a marriage.

By this time, I was starting to feel pressured and seeing things in his personality that made me a little concerned. Still acting based on his initial statement, "God says you're my wife," I never questioned anything. I just continued on the path we were on. One thing I can say, he was very open about his past and the baggage he would be bringing into the marriage. All of which should have been enough information for me to quickly get out of this relationship. You may ask, "Exactly how many red lights does God have to show you before you realize that Houston we have a problem?" Well, clearly my ability to see and hear had taken a back seat to my fleshly desires.

I remember one of my co-workers came to me one day and asked, "Does he have anger issues?" I pretended not to know what she was referring to, but I knew she had seen what I had witnessed personally, but was too embarrassed to share. That was the beginning of my voice being silenced. I didn't want anyone to think badly of him.

Not only did he have anger issues, he showed signs of being very possessive, controlling and domineering. Again, in spite of what I saw or experienced, I held onto his belief that I was his wife. How could I walk away from my blessing? If he is who God has for me, God will change him, right? Lesson to be learned, "what you birth in the flesh, you must maintain in the flesh." and what is birthed in the spirit, God will maintain by the spirit. What we had going on was ALL flesh in my opinion.

So, here I was in my little perfect Christian life, living with my fiancée, agreeing to take care of his disabled mother and about to take on the responsibility of taking care of his children for their first summer visit since his divorce. We were in a new apartment, I was overwhelmed and starting to get really concerned about the choices that I had made and we weren't even married yet. I had taken on more than I bargained for and he was asking me to assume even more responsibility for one of his sons, whom he wanted to bring to Florida to live with us. Finally, I spoke up. I was not down with that and I told him so. He got so angry with me. He started shutting me out; giving me the silent treatment and much to my dismay, he started having private conversations on the phone with a young lady. I discovered that by accident. I came home one evening to a locked door. I knew he was home but he wouldn't answer the door. When I finally got in, I heard him on the phone and it was very clear he was already setting up the next victim.

For me, that was the straw that broke this camel's back. I was hurt, angry and disappointed. The next day, I left work early and went to the apartment to pack all my stuff. I apologized and said goodbye to his mom and went back home. I only stayed with my sister a short while before I decided to get my own apartment. I was blessed to have found an affordable place, very close to my job. Things were starting to get back to "my normal." My sisters seemed a little concerned about my decision. That's because they had no idea what I had been dealing with. Months had passed and I didn't hear a thing from him until... I received a phone call one night after coming home from Bible study. It was him. Supposedly just calling to see how I was doing. I entertained the conversation even though my first response was not to answer. I did miss him very much but, somehow I knew if I answered the phone, I wouldn't be able to ignore him.

For some reason, he felt it necessary to share with me how well he was doing as if making a case for himself. We talked briefly and he shared with me that he felt led to call me (here we go again). The next thing I know, he felt led to show up at our Wednesday night Bible study. I instantly felt a sense that I needed protection, but I greeted him with kindness. I saw the look on Pastor Diana Lynn's face which was not one of pleasure. I could see that she was visibly concerned for me. I had shared with her while we were dating, that he was trying to pull me away from the church, which I was definitely not happy about. So the real "mama bear" in her was on high alert.

She and I had several counseling sessions after we split that were eye openers. She told me that he was a "counterfeit." When she said that, it made perfect sense to me. One of the young ladies in bible study prophesied what I knew to be a word of warning. She said that often times the enemy will bring you something that looks like its God but it's not and further explained how we need to be careful not to be deceived.

As soon as she said it, I wondered if she was talking about me. Of course I rationalized her words and thought to myself, "it can't be me, God said I'm his wife."

All Satan needs is an open door, then he pounces on the opportunity. That night, when I greeted him with a hug, I opened the door for him to walk right back into my life. Honestly, I knew then and I know now, it was never his intent to hurt me in anyway. We met at a time when he was in a very bad place emotionally and being alone with his own thoughts was more than he could handle. He was reaching out for the wrong thing; a new relationship, assuming that someone other than God could fill that void. Neither of us could see he was being used by Satan and we both were instruments in his plan to silence my voice and derail me from the path God intended for me.

I think Diana Lynn saw what was about to happen, but she couldn't interrupt the plan of God. This was a lesson I was going to have to learn from. I was clearly going to ultimately marry him in spite of what God and others had shown me. She saw the good in him as I had, but by the Spirit, she also saw the deep wounds and knew that he would never be whole until he allowed God to penetrate those places in his heart where he had been wounded and broken as a child.

There were a few times in Bible study that he was not slain in the spirit. So I knew for myself, that there was something very painful that God was trying to deliver him from. It may have actually happened for him had we both realized we needed to be nothing more than friends to one another. The lesson in all of this for me was, "know the Holy Spirit's voice for yourself and follow the sound counsel of those that God puts in your life." There is safety in a multitude of counsel, but it only works if your heart is open to receive it.

CHAPTER 8
To Hell and Back

Not long after we married, it became clear to me that my husband's response to stress and life challenges (particularly financial) caused him to act outside of his outwardly loving and gentle character. Unfortunately for me, his issues created a pattern that repeated over and over again. His anger and rage became more and more intense with each crisis. I became his object of retaliation. And like Job, the thing I feared the most had come upon me. One Sunday morning, as I was preparing for church, he became angry and told me I could no longer attend our church and he expected me to quit my job. He had already quit, so his excuse was, you cannot serve two masters. What the heck did that mean? I knew the bible interpretation, but that made no sense in the context that he was using it. The real answer was that he didn't want me around anyone else that could speak into my life; someone that may be able to see him for what he really was, namely Pastor Diana Lynn. I was heartbroken and confused.

His emotions were up one day and down the next. We shared a number of tender moments. One day after he came home from work, he held my face in his hands and said, "Skippy everything is going to be okay. I am going to take care of you. You don't have to work". After speaking these words, I looked up and saw tears in his eyes and he looked at me as though he saw something. Then he said, "God says, tell him what you want". I started crying and responded, "a happy marriage." Well, that fell on deaf ears I guess, but it was still a beautiful exchange and representation of the type of person he really was or desired to be deep inside, when he wasn't wrestling with the enemy.

I have always been a quiet person; not overly confident but I did manage to speak up for myself when necessary, as an adult. So, when he was verbally abuse towards me, my reaction was to express myself. However, I was quickly told that if I was going to speak, it had better not be anything negative against him. It was clear to me that from that point on, the dialogue was going to be one way only... and his way. So, in fear of his reaction, I shut down completely. What was the point in speaking if I couldn't do it freely or without being judged, criticized or corrected? Once again, my voice had been silenced, but this time as a means of protection. In the early stages of my marriage, I had allowed him to completely break my spirit.

Before I move any further, let me share something that I learned in my marriage that may hopefully save you from getting involved in an unhealthy relationship or worse, one that is not God ordained. I shared the things I'd been experiencing in my marriage with my friend, Patricia, a friend and she said, "Freda, it sounds like he has a Jezebel Spirit..." I didn't really know much about that, so I took the time to study it. Here is what one resource revealed about the "characteristics" of the Jezebel Spirit in a man (the characteristics in bold is what I personally experienced with him):

1. **He comes on strong, sweeping his victims off their feet. He can be a "hot, passionate lover." Women are flattered by his intense attention of them, and excited by his male dominant approach to sex**. He sexually "adores" them in a Romeo fashion or to be more up to date...**he speaks within KINGLY terms.**

2. He targets them by falsely mirroring their values, interests, goals, philosophies, tastes and habits. He is "everything you are." Wow, you have so much in common! You are THE PERFECT MATCH! He will ask where have you been all of his life. **He knows the right things to say, not to mention that you have been waiting for your Boaz to come through that door. Guess what? HE TELLS YOU THAT THE SET TIME HAS COME! TIMING SEEMS SO RIGHT....BUT <u>YOU WILL FIND OUT, IT IS SO WRONG AND NOT GOD!</u>**

3. **He fakes integrity, honesty and sincerity**. He convincingly mimics human emotions. He uses people. He is a "sincere liar."

4. **He can seem very spiritual or idealistic, but this is <u>superficial</u>. His interpretation of scripture, however, may not agree with what God had in mind.**

5. He can suddenly play the role of the victim. Similar to the <u>sneaky charming Jezebel</u>. Victims take pity on him. They see him as needing them. He is playing on the natural nurturing character of women.

6. He can inspire the woman to attack those who are supposed to be victimizing him. This causes injury to innocent people, and hurts the woman's relationships with others. **Her friends and family can be <u>ALIENATED</u> from her in this way.**

7. **He wants to marry victims quickly. <u>Impulsive</u>! He wants his victim dependent on him. He portrays <u>FALSE</u> integrity, appears helpful, comforting and generous.**

8. **The fake sincerity does not last as he starts to change into his true self. He will have numerous romantic relationships. He has no loyalty to anyone except his own body parts**.

9. **He blames others in the relationship**. His victims are <u>objectified and disposable</u>.

10. **His <u>lack of conscience</u> is shocking, incomprehensible and emotionally painful to the victim. He can suddenly end the relationship, without any compassion. The woman victim is <u>quickly discarded</u> as he cultivates a "new perfect partner." Or she may be able to end the relationship, and salvage what she can.**

11. **He may drop verbal clues about his true character early in the relationship, but victims**

fail to grasp its meaning. He romances them as he romances others, to exploit what stimulation he can get out of each one of them. Victims are too enraptured with all the physical or sexual attention, to realize that is all he is giving them is <u>words without substance</u>.

12. **Eventually the unmasked Jezebel emerges. His targets suffer emotional and financial devastation and their emotional recovery is lengthy.**

13. **He will recruit others as <u>he condemns you</u> for being a failure to him. Expect people he knows to <u>gang up</u> on you.**

14**. Nothing is his fault!**

15. **You can suffer and die, and he will not care. Maybe he will "pray" for you. This is insulting, at the least**.

16. In a church setting, he can be the perfect Christian. Everyone will idolize him and promote him; especially his new converts that don't even think twice to do a background check on him. **By the time they find out about his extra sexual (perverted) activities they will be <u>EMOTIONALLY and MENTALLY SOUL-TIED</u> to him. He may end up as an Apostle, Pastor or Leader under his own ministry with women that serve him** with an undying loyalty. Don't be surprised if he has not slept with most of them that are under his covering. He is so charming that everyone is impressed with him. He is a lady's

man, and the kind of man that women secretly admire and they will not reveal his attraction to them because he has already seduced them as bait.

17. When you start having problems with him, he will have the church "pray for you." **He is projecting his sin onto you, and condescending to you.** You will be the sinner, lost, and in need of deliverance, not him. **He has the <u>demon</u>, but you will get the bad reputation. He slanders successfully.**

18. The Jezebel man is not an <u>Ahab</u>. **The Jezebel is a <u>spirit of control and rebellion</u>.** The devil comes to steal, kill, and destroy. The Ahab is a permissive spirit that just lets the devil have his way.

19. **Jezebels are cruel, dishonest, <u>controlling</u> and critical, when they show their true colors.**

(<u>http://www.propheciesofrevelation.org/jezebel14.html</u>)

As I read this, I discovered how much of a passive personality I must have had based on the descriptions related to the characteristics of Ahab (Jezebel's husband in the bible). This was a most interesting find, so I share this as well to enlighten you:

1. Over-merciful vs. **over-legalistic:**
Passive people like Ahab tend to be over merciful, seeing the best in every person and overlooking too much. They forgive others too quickly (not making them aware of their offense) and also forgive people

who have not asked for forgiveness and are not even remorseful. This almost certainly guarantees the abuser's continued behavior. Aggressive people like Jezebel are on the other extreme — harsh in their expectations and unforgiving when people do not meet their unrealistic expectations.

2. Walking away from a person vs. walking over a person:

People with passive Ahab personalities quickly give away their power and walk away in order to avoid conflict. They find it easier to push their feelings inside. On the other hand, people with aggressive personalities seem to have no concern or conscience about whom they step on and use, as long as they get their way.

3. Avoiding confrontation vs. in-your-face confrontation:

Passive people avoid confrontation at all costs and will even blame themselves when others insult or betray them. However, aggressive people have no problem handing out insults and pushing blame on whomever they happen to choose. They have no regard for others' feelings, and will more or less tell you this.

4. Peacekeepers vs. peacemakers:

Passive personalities are notorious for being peacekeepers. They want the temporary, immediate gratification of keeping the peace at any price rather than "making peace" by boldly dealing with the issues at hand, which would result in more permanent, long-term gratification.

Freda N. Smith

5. Grumbling under one's breath vs. open verbal abuse:

People with passive personalities will resent verbal assaults, but they will refuse to take the offender to task and stop the behavior. Instead, they usually walk away grumbling. Aggressive people feel free to openly vent, abuse others and tell them off. Just minutes later, they will act as if nothing happened, even though they have left resentful people with wounded hearts in their wake. Jezebel personalities are so self-centered that they do not even realize they have severely damaged the people who happened to be in their destructive path, Ahab personalities leave others feeling responsible for them as victims.

6. Do not mind being wrong (if you'll approve of me) vs. refusing ever to be wrong (I'll love you if you see things my way):

Passive people often have such a need for approval that they will take the blame for anything if they perceive it as winning them your acceptance. Aggressive people will love you until you disagree with them! Then that love becomes a destructive hatred for you, and they will even go to the point of trying to destroy you and your reputation.

7. Fear of non-acceptance vs. fear of rejection:

While passive people will do almost anything to gain acceptance, aggressive people (who are always insecure and often wounded people) have a huge fear of rejection. Their actions come out of an "attack mode" because they are determined never to experience rejection again.

8. Low self-esteem (clothed in nice) vs. low self-esteem (clothed in fear of more hurt):

Passive people are usually nice people — too nice. They have low self-worth and try to gain ground by winning acceptance. Aggressive people also have low self-esteem, but usually they are bold, arrogant and pushy — all in an effort (because of old wounds) to avoid more hurt.

9. Fear of what people think of me vs. fear of people not agreeing with me:

The fear of man totally binds most passive people. They spend amazing amounts of energy trying to please everyone — even those they do not know or those who could not care less about them. Aggressive individuals, on the other hand, are so insecure that they see anyone who chooses to disagree with them as the enemy. Filled with their own insecurities, aggressive people perceive any type of correction as more rejection.

10. Anger directed inward vs. anger toward others:

Passive people are notorious for directing anger and insults back at themselves. If something goes wrong, they blame themselves. They often have major anger issues and will ultimately become passive-aggressive. Aggressive people pour their anger out on anyone who is available. They rarely look at themselves because they are so convinced that they are right. These aggressive personalities are self-appointed figures who think that it's their roles to correct the rest of the world. They are sarcastically referred to as "gods in training."

11. Accepting blame too easily vs. projecting blame (you made me do it):

Typically, passive people will quickly embrace blame in a situation in order to put everyone else at ease. While this is actually a kind of a false humility, passive people have the goal of making everyone happy again in order to increase their own self-worth. Like Jezebel, aggressive people will take blame for nothing! Even when caught in a wrong, their defense is, "You made me do it." "Yes, I robbed the bank, but it's your fault because you didn't give me enough money..."

This information may seem lengthy, but my intent is to share whatever I can to help others avoid the pitfalls that I stepped into. Remember the Bible says, "We are destroyed by a lack of knowledge". As you continue to read through these pages, you will see for yourself why I was amazed by my findings in this area. When I read it, I could almost picture my husband's face. Wow, if I had only listened. I cannot blame him for what happened in our marriage. People can only do to you what you allow. I allowed myself to be verbally abused, deceived, manipulated and controlled. I pray you don't make the same mistake in your marriage and/or relationship. Learn to value the exceptional person that you are... the one God says you are.

In my situation, when the finances were good so, were we; when it wasn't, all hell broke loose in our home. I longed for the person I thought I married. Where was the person that made me laugh; the one that made me feel like no one else mattered to him but me; the one that appeared strong and confident; the one that made my heart smile whenever he laughed? The man I lay next to each night had become harsh, cold and insensitive. Perhaps he realized he had made a mistake in marrying me. I actually wondered about that the day we went to the courthouse to get married. His hands were trembling so badly that his signature was unrecognizable.

After dealing with so much frustration on his job, coupled with the stress of having two baby mamas, he came to me to discuss quitting his job. At this point, I had no job and the only resources I had was investment funds from the sale of my home in Virginia. In my mind, this was the last thing in the world he needed to do with a new wife, child support and alimony payments due. I listened and then I agreed; for me to have any hope of peace, there was no other recourse. It was that or suffer even greater and I didn't want to see what that was going to look like. What would he do if I told him how I really felt? How are we supposed to live? How are you going to take care of your financial responsibilities outside of me? He was already financially unstable, knee deep in debt and I had no job at all.

Before we were married, he told me that I could leave my job because he could handle it… That was a lie from the pit of hell. Looking back, it wasn't about trusting him to provide for us. His intent was to have complete control over me and disable my ability to care for myself. At the same time, he felt the need to distance me from the ministry that he walked away from, that I was deeply connected to.

The next unintelligent decision came with his decision to go into full-time ministry and start a business that he said the "Holy Spirit" had given him the okay to do. Anytime he said Holy Spirit said anything, I didn't doubt or question it. I went along with it, hoping for the best. Though what felt to be like total manipulation in his efforts to persuade me, I used my investment funds to start the business and that's what we lived off of after he quit his job.

Again, I had already learned the hard way, not to speak anything against him. So here we are... newlyweds, unemployed and about to go into ministry and start a business with the last of my life savings.

My life was quickly spiraling out of control and I saw no way of escape. No matter how bad things got, and they did get much worse, divorce was never an option for me. Did I want to walk away? Yes, many times I thought about it, but my love for him and my empathetic nature for what I knew was driving his behavior didn't allow me to give up. I refused to give up! I loved him with all my heart and I thought loving him would be enough to support and inspire him to deal with the underlying issues that he refused to acknowledge. I wanted to fix him, but you can't fix someone that doesn't think they are broken, not to mention that no matter how much we love someone, it is the work of the

"Holy Spirit" to heal and transform lives. During a very low period, not long after we were married, he actually confessed to me that he didn't love himself and couldn't understand how I could love him. I was so broken at that point that I couldn't even respond. I think sometimes people feel safer in their place of pain because it's familiar. There was so much I could have said that might have made a difference in our marriage but when a person is not open or willing to confront the issues (past or present) there is nothing anyone can do. Sometimes what is not spoken is just as harmful as what is spoken.

He continued to make plans to start the business and I became the financial investor. He was excited to shared with the family what we were about to do. I was shaky about the ministry, but had grown to become hopeful about the business venture because I could see his excitement and passion and knew he had the creative and technical abilities to do well. The only thing he lacked was patience and wisdom through spiritual counsel. When he set his mind to do something, it had to be immediate. There was no planning involved, just make it happen by any means necessary and that's what we did.

Much to my surprise, the family seemed excited to support the idea of a ministry. We spent time looking for locations, but ultimately ended up holding services in our home. My spiritual mentor Diana Lynn used to say, "Right things done out of order and God's timing bring disastrous results." That's the direction we were headed in. Of course there is always something good that comes out of every trial. I will always be grateful for how God used him to bring several of my family members to Christ. He was certainly anointed to preach and was gifted in communicating. I listened to every message with a sense of pride, because I saw so much potential in him for greatness; I still do.

Our lives were a continuous emotional and financial roller coaster. Things always went well for a while. Soon the stress and fatigue of having a business, a ministry and kids to provide for became overwhelming. One of his great attributes was his love for his children and the responsibility he felt to provide for them. When he was not able to do that successfully, his pride was greatly wounded. The business took off faster than either of us expected and we were not prepared for the success. We were a staff of two. He was the primary producer - having to come up with designs, marketing strategies and materials, handle the production of goods as well as maintenance of the equipment. I was the administrative arm of the business and responsible for supplies and distribution of product. Looking back, I think that was God's way of showing us that the blessing is there but you have to be in order and we certainly were not. Anyway, the pressure of getting orders processed and mailed on a timely schedule took its toll on both of us physically and emotionally. We didn't sleep, seldom ate and had no time for each other. I remember one occasion that we had not slept in days. I had to drive to Tampa for supplies and apparently, I fell asleep behind the wheel. Thank God, nothing bad happened as a result.

It was all work and ministry. I personally started to hate it because of what I knew it was doing to us. Our marriage was already shaky and this, in my opinion, made a strained environment worse. All this work and further division in our marriage wasn't worth it financially. We were making good money for a mom and pop shop, but we were also spending a lot to get it done. There was little profit to take care of our personal expenses, but we kept persevering.

In the meantime, the ministry was starting to show signs of weariness as well. Family and friends that had joined us were quietly disappearing. I'm certain it was obvious to them that things were not well with us. I suppose they were losing faith and becoming disturbed by what they were seeing and hearing. Everything was falling apart before my eyes. By the time it came to an end, there was only three of us remaining. I however was relieved for many reasons. I didn't want to come out each week pretending everything was okay when it was far from that. We were arguing and bickering all the time. He was beginning to take things out on me and my family. They had no idea the actions and words that were taking place behind closed doors. How can you minister to people that you cannot tolerate being around? He began to see my family as the enemy when at one time he loved being with them. His actions were in direct response to that spirit of control. It was his way or he wanted nothing to do with you, so I had to stand up and minister to others when I myself needed to be ministered to.

I recall one occasion when he started an argument with me right before service was to begin. While sitting on an exercise ball, he rolled towards me, cursed me (the two words he took great pleasure in hurling at me) and with his finger pointed in my face he said, "Normally I would apologize but I mean what I'm saying, and I have no intention on apologizing to you or God." There was such an evil look in his eyes that had become all too familiar. I was balling my eyes out and couldn't believe he still expected me to go downstairs and open up the service... but he did and I went. Trying to hold back my tears, I did it.

Finally, one day, God stepped in and shut it all down. The business went first and then the ministry. I was so relieved. For the first time in a very long time, I cried tears of joy because I knew the "hell" was finally over. In my eyes, this was a divine course correction and an opportunity to realign to God's will for both of us. Perhaps now, we could make a good life together with all the weight and pressure gone. I didn't care if we had to live on skid row, I just wanted my husband back and the life I had dreamed of having with him.

After the business had been dissolved, we were lying in bed, just thinking about all that we had gone through. I was shocked to hear him express his relief, but also disappointed that his dream was not completely realized. It was in those moments that I loved him the most; when he opened himself up and allowed himself to be vulnerable and just accept himself, and his life, for what it was.

Now we had to start thinking about what we were going to do next. We had no income, no profit from the business and my investment fund was wiped out. He tried other ways of making money; he constantly searched for job opportunities, but to no avail. He went back to developing computer software, hoping that might generate funds, but again to no avail. One thing about him, he never gave up on an idea. He pushed himself as far as any man could to provide for his family; a slacker he was not and I loved that about him.

Another crisis was on the horizon, pulling him into what I believe was a brief period of depression. We became reclusive. We didn't really have friends, just my family, and he was at the point where he definitely didn't want to be around them. We were quickly becoming roommates as opposed to husband and wife. He stayed in the room all day on the computer and I busied myself around the house to avoid conflict, or eruptions of rage and anger. We had the kids for the summer during this time and because of our finances or lack thereof, we had no idea how we were going to get the kids back home. When he emerged from the bedroom, he had a plan. He came up with the campaign, "Sell the Lexus to get to Texas!" Because he made the sacrifice of selling the business equipment, I didn't push back about selling my car even though it was not what I wanted to do. That would leave us with a vehicle that we couldn't pay for and me departing with the last of what I owned. After much discussion, we did it. We sold the car and other items in the house, which provided enough income for the trip and our living expenses for the next few months.

I was emotionally and physically spent by the time he drove the children back to Texas. I was praying he wasn't going to ask me to take that ride again. He didn't. I think he wanted time away as much as I wanted to be alone. When he came back, we shared a few quiet, relaxing days together, with no arguing or complaining. Unfortunately, peace was always short lived in our household. The weight of our situation had to be dealt with. Now we were really at a loss and something had to break.

We were going through a tumultuous season in our lives; tested and failed many times, but God still had his hand on us. When it was obvious nothing was happening on the job front, he started talking about leaving the area. I knew from the beginning of our marriage that one day he would make this declaration. Things were so bad in our marriage prior to this. One day, while I was sitting out on the porch, he came outside and told me he would understand if I wanted to leave. I looked at him, but never spoke a word. Perhaps he was looking to me to release him from a marriage that never should have been. When he told me his plans, I cried, not because of leaving, but because of all that he did trying to make things work and for all that we had personally lost. He had been diligently searching for work and then he told me that he had a phone interview for a job in Oklahoma. They wanted him to come out for a second interview, but with no promises of a job. So, we talked about it and he decided to do it but as a permanent move.

Interestingly, the night before, God woke me up and spoke to my spirit that this was coming and that I was supposed to stay in Florida and he was to go to Oklahoma alone. So, the next morning when he told me what he was planning to do, he said he didn't want me to go because he didn't know what was going to happen. He said he could brave the unknown but it would be hard for me. I didn't see it then, but I believe God was using this to separate us, but I wasn't listening.

The next day, we shared the plan with my sister Patrice, the only one he hadn't separated himself from. She thought that I should go, with the limited information she had. Had she known what I had been going through, she would have told me to run and get out while I still could, but it was settled! We were moving to Oklahoma with only the prospect of a job offer. Once again, I dismissed what I knew God had just spoken to me because I didn't want to leave my husband. I felt if he went alone, I would never see him again. My heart was breaking at the thought of being apart in spite of all I had already endured in our marriage.

After the decision had been agreed upon, we made plans to vacate. We sold what we could and packed up only our personal belongings and the one remaining item from the business that hadn't been sold. He sent me to my mom's to say my final goodbyes to my family. It was a very unpleasant farewell. To their defense, they were horrified that I was leaving with him based on what they had seen and experienced. So unbeknownst to me, they had planned an intervention to keep me there. I was expecting to kiss them and say goodbye and be done with it, but that's not what happened. I was accused by my mother of taking money from the church, as well as, not paying back money I had borrowed from my sister. I was told I had been brainwashed and then the ultimate move… my sister Amber blocking me from exiting the house. I had to threaten her to move. I knew their hearts were in the right place. If I didn't know anything else, I knew my family loved me and everything they were saying and doing was out of great concern for my well-being but I hoped that they would see that I was doing what I thought I should do as a wife… but they didn't.

It made sense to me later that God was trying to keep me from being disobedient and getting myself into an even worse situation by any means necessary. I was so utterly wounded when I left, I drove straight to Patrice's home. She sat in the car with me trying to console the heaviness in my heart. As I tried to control my tears.

I couldn't go back home in the shape I was in because I was fearful of what his response might be. Patrice listened quietly, offered advice and we parted ways. When I got home, I'm sure he could see that I had been crying but he was very calm and just asked me how it went. He comforted me as much as he could and let it go.

The next morning, was "D" day. All that was left to do was for him to say goodbye to his sister. She came and gave us some money for the trip and then we left. We had roughly eight-hundred dollars to live off of and only the hope of a full-time job when we arrived in Oklahoma. Not much was said, pulling out, because I could not contain my tears. I was leaving absolutely EVERYTHING that was familiar to me to go to a place where I had no support and no promise that things would be any different. He was being obedient to the "Holy Spirit's" direction for his life, but I was in total disobedience. I was about to feel the sting of my poor decisions.

As I recall, we arrived in Oklahoma a night or two before his interview. When we arrived, we were both exhausted, so we looked for a place to lodge for the night. We found something we could afford, but dear Lord, it was the worst looking hotel I'd ever been in and creepy too. We both felt the presence of spirits in that place. It was a demonic hot spot. The next day, we decided to drive to the interview location just to make sure we knew where to go the day of his interview. As we left, we drove by a place called "Mercy Ministries." We saw all the people standing outside and decided we'd check it out. Upon entering the facility, we knew immediately God was surely with us. We waited around for the director of this organization to speak with us.

Rosa was the kindest person I'd met in a very long time and was more than welcoming. We shared our situation with her and she quickly mobilized people to help us out with needed supplies. I felt so relieved and I know my husband did as well. God's favor was more real to me than ever at that moment. In addition to supplies, she gave us the name of someone that just so happened to need that one piece of equipment we brought with us. That's what you call Favor!

At this point, we had very little money left, so this was yet another extreme blessing. Only God could set something like that up. We met with the business owner and with no questions he purchased the machine even though when we got it there, it would not work! "Are you kidding me?" My husband was beyond himself, but neither of us lost hope. These people seemed to sense our honesty, faith and desperation. Such kindness was just unbelievable. They were able to get the machine running and we now had enough cash to get into a safe and clean motel. We drove around quite some time looking for something close, but affordable.

In spite of the struggles and being in unfamiliar territory, I was glad to be taking this journey with my husband. I believed with all my heart that once we got settled things would be good for us. The interview went well and thank you Jesus, he got the job. I knew in my heart that God would not abandon us. Of course, he had to begin work knowing that he would not get a paycheck for a couple of weeks. Now what do we do? Well, God already had a ram in the bush and her name was "Rosa."

When my husband started his new job, I would ride in with him and go volunteer at the mission outreach. I was so excited to be serving in ministry again and have the opportunity to be around my new friend Rosa and the other volunteers. It was far greater than being in a hotel by myself. Rosa and I grew close very fast. She shared her story with me and I shared mine with her. She immediately kicked into high gear trying to find a living arrangement for us knowing that we really couldn't afford to remain in hotels. She ultimately worked out a temporary living arrangement for us that worked out perfectly. We had food and shelter at no expense to us and if my husband chose to, he could have walked to his job. Rosa and her family openly embraced us with the love of God in ways I could not have imagined.

Things were better, but my husband still seemed to be on edge and stressed most of the time. I just worked at trying to keep the peace between us and keep my own sanity. I found that I really didn't miss my family as much as I thought I would. I actually enjoyed the independence and having relationships outside of family for a change. Our friends at the missions had become my lifeline outside of my relationship with the Lord.

The next task was trying to find a local church. We visited one that my husband felt led to try, but he quickly realized that was not THE place. One of the volunteers asked us to visit his church on a night of revival. It was an old style Baptist church, but quaint and friendly. That night they had a guest speaker. He was older, but on fire for the Lord. I enjoyed his preaching and so did my husband. We stayed behind after the service to introduce ourselves to him. It was very clear that this was another "God" intervention. It was a divine setup.

I felt a spiritual connection; fatherly closeness to him right away. When he spoke with my husband, he gave him a word that I will never forget. He told my husband that it was very important that he make me feel safe and secure. I burst into tears. He didn't know us, but he was reading my mind. I remember thinking, "he's not listening to you."

After visiting this church only once, we ended up visiting one of the largest church organizations in Oklahoma called Life Church. It was different than any place I'd ever been. Different worship experience, environment and delivery of the word. I came to really enjoy it. Although they had many campuses, each of substantial size in congregation, they seemed like a very close knit family of believers.

Life continued to roll on, but things had begun to get very stressful on my husband's job. I could tell by the way he interacted with me that we were about to once again go through a rough spot. His rough spots always resulted in anger, rage and separation physically from me. I had finally begun to see his cycles for what they truly were. Things were good as long as he had no financial stress or "baby mama drama." It seems like we experienced one storm after another. When would we ever just be able to breathe? Every day, I had to be very aware of what I said, how I responded to him and what I did to prevent an emotional eruption. Whatever he was going through or feeling seemed to always be projected on to me in some way.

Then in one moment, my heart and my world was shattered. I went to pick my husband up from work and he told me I had to call home. My sister Patrice had contacted him to let me know my sister Lin had been diagnosed with Stage 4 Cancer and was in the hospital. My husband once told us that Lin was the "nucleus" in our family. What a revelation that was. I personally never thought of it in those terms, but her actions certainly exhibited that. She really was the glue that held us all together.

I was in shock, my heart was hurting, yet I was doing everything I could to hold back my tears in his presence. Why did I have to be so far away at a time like this? My husband knew how close our family was and my connection with Lin. I knew he had no love for my family so any words of comfort would fall on deaf ears. He just asked if I was okay. It was a silent ride home. When we arrived home we discussed it. He was concerned that I would be thrown back into a depression. Well, one thing I knew for sure, no matter what happened, I would never again allow myself to sink that low, ever! I was much stronger than he ever gave me credit for.

I guess he did the best he could to console me, but

at that point, I just wanted to be alone to try to make sense of what I'd just heard. My thoughts were on my family members and what I knew they were going through. The next day I spoke with my sister, Carolyn and she explained the situation with Lin. She said it had been stressful on them having to keep a twenty-four-hour vigil at the hospital and really wished I could get home. To my surprise, that night my husband told me after all I'd sacrificed for him; he wanted to use the limited money that we had to get me a plane ticket to go home. I wanted to be with my family desperately, but I knew we didn't have the resources and I had already determined that I was not going to ask based on past experiences and conversations we'd had about finances. The words he spoke to me before leaving Florida crept into my thoughts, "now don't expect to be able to run home every time something happens with your family." Was that even in the case of death, I wondered? My husband's heart had grown cold and angry with my family members before moving to Oklahoma. I really didn't expect him to understand what I was feeling. It didn't matter, I trusted God to intervene on my behalf and He did just that. Most of the time my husband was unpleasant to be around because of the things he was dealing with (or not dealing with personally) but there were always times when it seems God moved on his heart and he was very loving, sensitive and kind. This was one of those times.

So, I began to make plans. It was perfect timing, because he had just received his first paycheck. I knew this was a huge sacrifice for him because of his financial commitments to his children, so I was more than grateful. He also told me that he was okay with me being home for at least one month, but no longer, not knowing what the medical prognosis really was. Again, I was grateful he was willing to give me that time. That night, I was awakened out of my sleep by the Lord telling me that he was going to change his mind.

Driving into work the next day, he started making comments about me leaving him at the worst possible time. He talked about having to make the financial sacrifice when I knew we couldn't afford it and his displeasure with me in deciding to go. I could not believe what I was hearing even though the Holy Spirit had already prepared me. It had never been clearer to me than it was at that moment that he was allowing the enemy to work through him again. What else could it have been for someone to flip flop so easily and quickly? I believe his spirit man was in constant conflict with the Holy Spirit. What kind of turmoil was he really dealing with internally? It had to be awful and exhausting as well. When we got home, the night before my departure, he sat on the bed and told me that the Holy Spirit spoke to him and said that what was happening to my sister was a result of judgment. He said, "the thing she wished on him was coming back on her." He never shared what he believed she wished on him. He continued, "because of that, her life is being required of her." Now I knew the Holy Spirit did speak to him, but I also saw for myself that the voice that he heard was not always the Holy Spirit. Out of curiosity, I asked "why her and not anyone else?" His response, "because her soul is secure in heaven." Well, as I knew it, any of the one's that would have and probably did speak ill of him, were also saved and if that were the case, he'd be dead too, for all the ugly things that came out of his mouth about me and my family. I think I hated him at that moment for saying the most insensitive and evil thing he could. I just went silent and for a second, wondered if there could possibly be any truth in his words. I was disgusted with myself for even considering that to be true. At the same time, a weight of guilt came upon me. I thought to myself, "This would not have happened to her if I had never married him!" Jesus, was this as a result of my disobedience? Lin would not have EVER spoken harm to him or anyone else, even though I knew she was truly disappointed in what she was seeing in our marriage.

I was scheduled to leave the next morning. All I had to do was get through the night. I so needed him to console and hold me; to comfort me through the night, but like so many other nights, it never came. The morning of my departure was met with more opposition and spiritual attack.

I could sense darkness in the room; an unease and frustration in him. As fate would have it, when it was time for me to leave, the car would not start. I knew exactly what I was up against. I just sat and quietly prayed. He went on his computer in an attempt to troubleshoot the issue, but the computer was not operating properly. As was the case with most things that he went through or experienced, that became my fault.

God immediately stepped in again to make sure I got out of there. He suggested that I call my friend, Rosa to see if she could get me to the airport. She was my life saver. She quickly responded and was there in no time flat. That day, God was determined that, "no weapon formed against me, would prosper." I didn't realize at the time, but the intended few weeks trip to Florida, to be with Lin, would actually end up being a six-month separation in my marriage. I had no idea when I got on that plane the next morning, that it would be the last time I would see my husband for six months. I was due to come back right before the Christmas holiday.

I was in warfare mode for Lin's life from the moment I boarded the plane in Oklahoma. I wanted to go to her as soon as I landed in Florida, but because of her condition and the circumstance of her sickness, I had to wait until the next day.

My niece, Kim and I arrived in Tampa within 20 minutes of each other. We hadn't seen each other in well over a year and we were both there on a mission. One of the first things that she said to me was that the Holy Spirit spoke to her about Lin's position as well as about her condition. That night, we stayed together at Lin's house and stayed up late to talk and connect, knowing what we were about to face. This is what she told me as she explained her own personal struggles to make it there in time and what she was tasked to do.

The Holy Spirit said to Kim in the midst of an emotional breakdown, *"You are right, she is THE ONE! She is the Moses of this family. She has suffered silently, bearing the cross for the lost and troubled souls in this family and she needs to hear a specific message from me."* He went on to say, *"She needs to know that her suffering has not been in vain, that I have always been here with her. However, like Moses' staff had power, her staff was her voice and the enemy has silenced her voice because she had refused to use it."*

Kim began to take notes, realizing that this was too important to get the message wrong. The Holy Spirit continued, *"She has had something important to say for many years. She is sick because she is so afraid that speaking her heart will hurt certain people's feelings, therefore she has decided to bear the cross alone in silence. She doesn't understand that if she were to speak her heart, not only would she fully recover from this illness, but her words would break the chains of bondage off of this family."* Kim, like me, knew the bondage that God was referring to was the family's "code of silence".

She asked out loud, "and what do you expect me to do?" Holy Spirit's response was, *"I am not sending you down there to say goodbye and I am sending you down there to save her life. Tell her how much I love her and that she has a decision to make. Tell her that you all would learn more from her miraculous recovery than you would from her death."* The last thing God said was, *"Tell her that if she chooses to live, she has to choose to use her voice and speak her heart."*

That was deep, so we got prayed up and quietly prepared ourselves for what was to come next. We went to see her, early the next morning.

The moment I saw her lying in that bed, I was mad as hell at the devil. I walked over to her and of course she greeted me with a smile and asked me to thank my husband for getting me there. Wow, in all that she was going through, she still had a loving spirit about her. My niece Erica commented, "Well Lin, I guess this was your way of getting Auntie back home." As soon as she said it, I knew that's exactly what God had done. While He didn't create the situation, He used it to take me out of a bad situation. When I arrived in Florida, I contacted a friend of mine named Pastor Fred. He was from my former church and I asked him to come and pray for my sister. He arrived not long after I got there. I was grateful for the prayers. When he left, my sister asked me to sing one of her favorite gospel hymns, "Higher Ground." She lay there with her eyes closed. As I softly sang the words, I wondered what was going through her mind. Was she reflecting deeply on things we will never know about?

I could see in Lin's eyes that she was not expecting to survive this fight and she was preparing herself for death. My heart was aching for her. The words of faith I was speaking over her did not seem to penetrate. She just smiled as I spoke to her. Because of the "tracheotomy," her voice was not clear, but I could still understand her words. Her next request was that I call my husband to have him pray over her. That took me by surprise initially, but I knew there was something deeper stirring within her that was causing such a sense of urgency.

I personally didn't feel that his prayer would be genuine, but it wasn't about me, so I called. I don't know what he prayed, but she seemed to feel relieved as tears rolled down her face. She ended the conversation with a simple whisper, "thank you." As for me, I was rebuked for making contact with Pastor Fred – yet, still no compassion for what I was dealing with. So, I too said thank you and ended the call.

Lin then asked me a question that solidified what I had been asking myself regarding what was on her mind. She asked me to make sure I took care of Erica (her daughter). To be there for her because she knew she would not handle her death well. She also asked me to find George, Erica's estranged father and ask him to come to be with her. That was the first time to my knowledge, she EVER asked him to do anything concerning her. We could have prayed for her until the walls came down, but for Lin, it was already over. For whatever reason, she had given up all hope. She was holding on for Erica and no one else.

All the family from Virginia that could come to Florida, had arrived by this time. We paired up and sat with Lin twenty-four hours a day to watch over her. It was emotionally and sometimes physically draining, but we would not trade that time with her for anything. Lin's last few weeks in the hospital were immensely painful. She was unable to eat, speak, or sleep without being heavily medicated. Eventually, they put her in a coma like state just to keep her comfortable and to rest. One night, while I was with Lin, God gave me the most beautiful dream concerning her. In my dream, I was on the most beautiful beach, surrounded by a host of angels and precious jewels. It was the perfect depiction of who Lin was to me. It was such a place of serenity and peace that you could not imagine. I can still picture it in my mind today. Watching her, it seemed that Lin was already in Glory and it was only her body that remained here on earth. I know this dream was God's way of preparing me and giving me peace about her ultimate transition.

The day Lin passed, we were called to the hospital where we were gathered in a conference room to be updated. At this point, both Erica and I were still believing that there was a chance that she would live through this. Erica hadn't really prepared herself to receive what the truth actually revealed. Minutes later, the nurse came in and said that she was dying. We all ran back to her room, but it was too late...she was gone. The ventilator remained on making it appear that she was still breathing. I stood silently by her bedside praying that she would come back and watching for signs of life to prove that my prayers had been answered. How very selfish of me. She was now pain free!

Lin passed away on November 5, 2009 from

Anaplastic Thyroid Cancer. A type of cancer that is inherent in eighty-year-old white men, per her doctor. Despite the immensely painful radiation treatments that she endured for her daughter's sake, it did not save her nor prolong her life. I'm grateful that God, in all his love and mercy, did not allow her to suffer long. She passed away only a few short months after being diagnosed. To say that the entire family was shattered and in shock would have been an understatement.

Lin's love for her family was only surpassed by her great love for God! In everything she did, you could see God's heart in her. She gave her best at all times, whether it was helping her family, on the job or serving in her church. She was faithful in all things. Although I witnessed the pain and suffering my sister went through, I refused to believe that God was not going to heal her. Sometimes, in spite of believing, praying and fasting, God's answer is not what you expect. I was truly disappointed, deeply grieved and angry about her death, because I felt responsible for introducing Brian to her and everything that resulted from that. I wondered, had I not married him, would things have turned out different.

It wasn't so much that it was God's will, but Lin's desire to be with the Father. As she shared with my sister Patrice, "I love God with all of my heart, but I do not love this world." For Lin, I believe when faced with the choice to live and continue to experience the pressures and weights (physically and otherwise) of this life, or to be released from it all and spend eternity with the Lord, she chose based on her deep love for the Lord. "To be absent from the body, is to be in the presence of the Lord." To this day, that scripture is the only thing that gives me peace. As I write this passage, the song comes to mind, "may the works I've done speak for me." Lin, I'm sure they did and the words back to you had to be, "Well done, thy good and faithful servant. Enter into my blessed rest."

Ironically, while Lin was in the hospital, she was also visited by a lady that was a part of the hospital's chaplain services. She had just finished praying over her and was leaving the room as I arrived. First, she asked us how Lin's stomach had gotten so big? Then she asked us if Lin was a worshipper? We responded by sharing how much she loved to sing in the choir. It was then that she told us that there was something Lin was supposed to say, that she had been afraid to share. She shared this, never having met my niece Kim, and neither of us told anyone about what Kim said the Holy Spirit shared with her about the same thing to have justified the connection.

It's been seven years since she passed away and I still find it difficult to say the words, "She's dead." After the funeral services, everyone returned home to business as usual; except for me. I went home with Erica, so she would not be alone. Once the house was quiet, I phoned my husband. He seemed glad to speak with me, but when I started crying and trying to tell him how I was feeling, his response was, "I'm sorry, but I can't really offer you any comfort." Are you serious? How could anyone be so cold? Reflection: To protect His own, God can harden the heart of our oppressors to move us out of harm's way.

Erica had offered to purchase my ticket to get back home. I was anxious and excited to go back home until a conversation I had with my husband late one night. Our conversation was very pleasant initially and then in a split second, he turned on me. He shared with me that he thought it would be better for me to stay where I was. He was doing better without me and continued to remind me of the effect my leaving him (to come home for Lin) had been on his life. It was the guilt trip that had become very familiar to me. I didn't even consider it at the time, but as I write this, his real reason was probably more about his infidelity than anything. The way to release his guilt was to transfer it onto me. The next day we talked on the phone briefly, just long enough for him to tell me not to call him. After much prayer and many tears, I made up my mind to cancel my flight. That began the period of official separation and I went back to mama's house. After having no contact with him for several months, I called him to notify him of a piece of official mail, I received on his behalf. When he called me back, he said he had been praying about our situation and told God, "If she reaches out to me, then I will ask her to come back." I missed him terribly so when we did start talking by phone, it felt like it did when we first met. Hearing his voice always stirred something in my heart, to the point that I forgot about all of the bad! We talked, we laughed and of course, I cried. I had to face some facts about things that had transpired in my absence and decide whether or not I could live with some of his choices. In spite of what he shared, I chose to go back. I loved my husband and I desperately wanted to repair my marriage. I was on a plane headed back to Oklahoma before the end of April 2010.

He was living in a very comfortable two-bedroom apartment. It was perfect by my standards. The best feature was the huge lake behind the complex. It had a beautiful gazebo in the middle and a walking area that encircled it. It was my type of atmosphere. In the evenings, we walked around the lake and sat on the bench and talked as we watched the ducks swim by. I cherished those moments and relished the honesty and gentleness of his conversation. I felt loved and safe and I never wanted him to take his arms from around me. When he asked me if I was ready to go back to the house, I said no because I didn't want this moment to end. I knew he understood.

Unfortunately, within a couple of months or less, we were experiencing turmoil again. The one good thing was that we had a place to live and his job was pretty stable, but he had been seeking employment opportunities elsewhere. When he took the job in Oklahoma City, it wasn't paying anything near what his skill set was worth.

When I got back, I started volunteering again with the same mission outreach program. It was like I had never left. That was short lived, because he started to resent me being there and not being available to him when he needed me. From the time he got up in the morning and on the ride to and from work, he always found fault with me about something. Everything agitated him. I felt the stress and discomfort of living in the same house with him. The stress on his job was unbearable and I knew what that was going to lead to.

The kids were due to come out for spring break. He was always excited about visiting with them and did everything in his power to make things comfortable for them. However, due to the financial constraints, he made the decision to have them wait and come out for the usual summer break. This time, making the trip to pick up the kids was a breeze since we were only traveling from Oklahoma to Texas. Everything was good until the ride back home. We experienced a tire blowout in the middle of the night in the middle of nowhere. The kids were troopers. They endured the experience and we all thanked God for his watchful eye over us. We were able to get a tow into the nearest town. We got a hotel for one night and by morning, he had the tire repaired. I was so nervous; fearing that this would cause him to flip out, but he handled it fairly well and we arrived home safely with the kids.

We were all enjoying the summer and finding activities to occupy our time. We had family game nights that the kids really enjoyed. Soon after the stress of his job crept in again and he was just not happy at all. Weeks later he was terminated from his job. I knew that was going to be the beginning of the end. He was very upset, tired and weary of it all, I'm sure. I wanted to be there for him in any way that I could, but that wasn't what he wanted, to my dismay. He spent a lot of time alone in the room while the kids and I kept busy with outside activities. I knew he needed the quiet time and some space to figure things out so, I left him to himself. One night, while enjoying some family time with the kids, he emerged from the bedroom and walked up behind me and just hugged me. I relished that one moment of tender affection. The next morning, as I was preparing for church, he asked me what I was doing, and from the tone in his voice, I knew a rage was brewing. When I responded that I was getting ready for church, he made a comment about me dressing nice for church, but not caring about what I looked like for work. I was completely confused as this seemed to come from nowhere. Being fueled by his own words and my lack of response, he started cursing.

At that moment, something rose up inside of me and I could no longer hold my tongue. I dealt with this type of verbal abuse throughout our marriage and I was done! I turned to him and fired back, letting him know I was no longer going to allow him to speak to me like that. I told him that if he chose to use that language, he'd better do it with some other woman. He looked to be in shock that I had actually talked back to him. It wasn't me; it was the Spirit of God in me. Hallelujah, I got my voice back and never again would I allow my voice to be silenced by him or anyone else. I walked away and left him lying there and I proceeded to church without them.

In some ways, I think that taking a stance, although shocking was a relief to him. It certainly gave him a sense of justification for his own actions which only perpetuated his feeling of being in control and acting in a domineering manner. I tried to talk to him when I got home and he finally said IT.

From that day forward, he went into retreat mode from me and the kids. He spent hours in the bedroom on his computer. I had no idea what he was doing. One night, I had a horrible dream that woke me from my sleep. I dreamt that he was suffocating me with a pillow. That was the last time we slept in the same bed together. I moved out onto the couch. That gave him the perfect opportunity to continue to do his thing in secret. But, what you do in secret, God will bring to light and that was about to happen. My husband did not speak a single word to me for three weeks and I had little interaction with the kids. I took a walk one day, down to the lake and sat on that beautiful Gazebo directly in the middle of the lake. I began to pray and ask God for direction. I started to sing and the most beautiful thing happened. A family of ducks surrounded that Gazebo as if they were listening. I smiled and thanked God because I knew that was Him letting me know, He was with me. I had such a peace in my spirit after that.

The Holy Spirit began to reveal to me exactly what he was doing behind closed doors. He was disappearing from the house late at night (when everyone was asleep) or so he thought. He would take phone calls outside, away from the house.

Surely he didn't think I was that stupid. I waited, I prayed, I sought counsel. The word says, "There is safety in a multitude of counsel". I hated life, because I would not let myself believe he was cheating on me right under my nose. I heard him talking about me to another woman; expressing his desires to be with her. It was a nightly conversation only he had no clue I could hear him. It sickened me, but it also angered me enough to finally give up on things ever being what I dreamed they would be.

I tried to get him to talk, but it was clear he was not going to relinquish his stance of silence with me. He told me, "It would be best for me not to say anything to him". Even though things were not right with us, I continued to care for the kids and him. All his meals were served in the room. He never ate with me and the children. Completely to my surprise, one day he came out of the room and said one word, "Hi", in a condescending voice and with a smirk on his face as we passed each other in the kitchen. At that point, I had no words for him either.

To get through this season of silence, I chose to immerse myself in worship. It was the only way I knew to survive. And as if I was disturbing those spirits in him, he came storming out of the room, got right up in my face and told me to turn it down or use earphones. His eyes were red as fire. I looked right through them having a complete understanding of what was really facing me down. Not long after this incident, I received an email from him. Why an email you ask, when the only thing that separated us was a bedroom wall, I could not tell you. The email

Freda N. Smith

simply stated that he couldn't be married to me anymore. That he should have left me where I was in Florida (after my sister's death). He then says, "if I was not going to allow him to speak or share his opinion than he could not be my husband" (and by that he meant if you won't allow me to curse you out without you feeling the need to defend yourself then I can't be your husband). He said he wanted to talk whenever I was ready. Me ready, are you kidding?

I had no desire to prolong this mess any longer. He actually had the nerve to tell me that there would be nothing I could say or do to change his mind. That was surely not my plan. That evening, he emerged from the dungeon and with a smile on his face, asked me how I was doing. I was dealing with some serious demonic spirits. I listened as he spoke (which was typically our communication style). I had only one question. I asked just out of curiosity of what his response would be, "How am I supposed to get home?" His response was, "I'm not using my money to get you home." Maybe get a job or call someone in your family," he continued. I had to smile inside myself when what I really wanted to do was strangle him for his arrogance and insensitivity. Through our marriage I had made ultimate sacrifices financially to support his dreams and I ended up penniless. Now he had the nerve to tell me to get home the best way I knew how.

He seemed to be reveling in this moment. For me, it was confirmation of what God had shown me. He was releasing me from this marriage. I did as he suggested, knowing that I would have a ticket out of that place immediately with one phone call home. He was making arrangements to get the kids back home. The day before they left, he called the children into the room very late. He assumed I was asleep on the couch (as usual). I heard him tell them that we were not going to be together. He told me he would not have that conversation without me, but he did. His version beautifully covered up the truth. I heard one of the children crying. When they came out of the room they came over to the couch and hugged me. My heart was breaking for them. They had seen so much turmoil in their dad's life and were exposed to more mess than they should have been.

In my times of isolation, it became clear to me that he could not bear the quietness of being alone; wrestling with his own thoughts and being tormented by his past. I came to that conclusion (and yes, it's my opinion), after watching him in the two years we were together. In that moment, I was reminded of what he had spoken before. He once shared with me that he couldn't understand how I loved him when he didn't even love himself. That was an eye opener for me at the time he confessed it and I believe the result of his decision to end our marriage further confirmed it. I sat on the couch that night and prayed for whom ever the other woman was. I prayed that God would protect her from being taken in by this deeply wounded man. It is true what they say, hurt people hurt other people.

The next morning, I left the house as they were

preparing to go. I knew I could not bear to see them drive away. While I still had my composure, I went out to the car to tell each one of them how much I loved them and that I was sorry. I really loved those kids and I wanted to give them a loving, nurturing and healthy home life and I had failed. When I couldn't hold back my tears any longer, I returned to my place of peace and solace.... the lake. I stayed there until I knew they were gone. That was the last time I saw my husband. While he was gone, I made arrangements for my friend from the missions to come get me. I cleaned up the apartment, packed my bags and sat down to write him. After writing my thoughts and feelings in the letter, I left it on the bed and walked away.

The day he left with the kids, I was not aware of his plan to go home to Cleveland (this I discovered thru social media). I knew approximately how long it would take him to drive to Cleveland and back. Knowing that, I had to quickly figure out a way to get out of that apartment until it was time for me to depart Oklahoma and head back home.

I knew I would not be able to handle being there when he got back home. Before he left, he was kind enough to tell me I could stay there until I got enough money to leave. That night, I took off on foot, roaming the highway for a pay phone to call my friend Rosa from the missions. The whole time I'm walking the dark streets, I'm talking to myself wondering what the heck I was doing out there alone in an area that I was certainly not familiar with. Anything could have happened to me and no one would have known… But God. I finally got the nerve to walk into one of the hotels nearby that had a phone in the lobby (nothing but God). I waited outside for a moment to take note of the layout and for the people inside to leave; noticing that the phone was out of view of the front desk. I walked in finally and acted as though I was a guest, just hanging out in the waiting area.

I called my friend several times and there was no response. Dear Jesus! I was at a loss for what to do next. I refused to give up and at that point I had no other options. So as not to be noticed, I walked back to the apartment after leaving her several messages. After an hour or so, I went back out and returned to the hotel. This time I was able to reach Rosa and she quickly responded to my desperate plea for help. She and her husband were so thoughtful and kind to welcome me into their home; even giving me my own room in the hopes I would consider staying in Oklahoma. I knew I was not interested in doing that. I needed to get home. I stayed with them for about two weeks; helping them get their new home together. I enjoyed every moment because it helped me take my mind off of what was going on in my own life. When I wasn't helping her at home, I'd go to work with her and help with the mission's outreach. God always gives us opportunities to be a blessing; I hope I was to them, just as they had been to me.

The day finally arrived. For the second time I was walking away from a place I thought would be home but ended up being a temporary holding spot.

I guess I should have been grateful that God did not delay the inevitable. One thing about my character is that I have always found it difficult to give up on people, but this time I had no choice. My only comfort in leaving was that I knew in my heart, I had done everything I could to save my marriage. I said good bye to my dear friend at the airport. As the plane took off, I felt a wave of emotion and a hurt in my heart that seemed unbearable. I have never felt as defeated and utterly alone as I did in that very moment. When I could no longer contain my tears, I put my head down with my face to the window and let it all out. Thank goodness no one was sitting beside me.

My sincere prayer concerning my husband was to see him get to a point in his life where he confronts his past, is honest with himself and God and to allow the Holy Spirit to heal him in every place that he has been wounded, rejected and violated. I have always and will always wish God's best for him and his family and that will never change.

When I arrived at the airport in Virginia, I was drained emotionally. I tried to muster up a smile as I was lovingly welcomed home by my sister, Carolyn. I realized how good God was in the wealth of love and compassion that my family showed me during my stay. At the time, I had no idea if this was going to be my permanent home or another temporary holding pattern. A holding pattern is exactly where God had me. I had nothing but the one suitcase of personal items and clothing. My first weekend home, one of my brothers picked me up and took me shopping telling me to get whatever I needed. I was overwhelmed by the generosity and felt guilty for even having the need. I graciously accepted his gift.

My husband was right, my family would always be there for me, but that is just how we are. I think that's what he disliked most about them. He seemed resentful at times about the closeness I had with my family and the fact that we were ALWAYS there for one another.

The week I arrived in Virginia, my sister, Patrice was scheduled to arrive for a brief vacation. It was perfect timing because I had not seen her since I left Florida. It was a mini reunion. As much as I was hurting, it was a great relief to be around others in my family doing what we all loved most - hanging out, laughing, sharing memories and eating all kinds of good food.

Carolyn did her absolute best to console me and be there for me emotionally, but I honestly just couldn't articulate what I was feeling. She always respected my need for solace, yet she always let me know that she was there if I needed her. I don't know how I would have gotten through those times without her and the love and support of my brothers.

As my mentor Diana Lynn shared with me, it was time for me to let others take care of me instead of me being the one trying to take care of everyone else. That was not an easy thing for me then or now, but I'm learning. I never connected with a ministry while in Virginia. One weekend my niece, Kim and I traveled to Baltimore for a service from one of my favorite TV Pastors, Dr. Jamal Harrison-Bryant. Kim had just written her first book telling her personal story and felt led to give it to him. Neither of us knew the impact that service would have on us. During the service, he called people out that had been going through challenging situations to come to the altar and just cry out to God. I felt a little reserved initially, but she and I folded arms and went together. Much to my amazement, I let it all go at that altar. Every repressed emotion, hurt, anger etc., just flooded out of me with the most blood curtailing screams. Was this me? It was the Holy Spirit emptying me out so He could heal those wounded places to prepare me for a fresh infilling of His Spirit and God knows I needed that to move forward. When we left that conference, I felt like the life force had been drained out of me. I could barely walk. I was so weak and I had almost completely lost my voice, but it was worth it.

The days following, I immersed myself in the word, praying, fasting and watching online services of Bishop TD Jakes. God spoke powerfully in those quiet times in my sister's home office. God opened my eyes and my heart and revealed himself to me in ways I could not have imagined. My time in Virginia was a place of healing and regrouping for the ultimate plan he had for me... a complete Exodus from one place of existence to coming full-circle. When I knew it was time to move on, I knew my family, especially Carolyn, (which I felt horrible for leaving her) was going to be sad. I felt all along that this was not my "place called there" (a phrase my husband used when he made reference to OKC, which I believed in). God had a specific assignment for me and that came with me being positioned where He chose. Not my will Father, but your will be done!

There was no communication between my husband and I for a long time until one day I received a message from him asking me for my mailing address. As hurt as I was, I simply could not be angry with him. Our conversation was cordial and polite. On one occasion he actually apologized to me for not being a good husband. I apologized to him as well for anything I had said or done that hurt him. Conversations with him only reminded me of the marriage I desired, but never had with him. I still loved him so deeply and it still did something to my heart whenever I heard him laugh. That's when I always knew, he was okay. Then, I started seeing Facebook posts that really angered me. One in particular caused me to react and I called him to question him about it. I was furious that he would be publicly sharing about a relationship that he was in and it was more than hurtful to see expressions of love towards him from another woman. Did he forget we were still married? I was to find out later, according to him, it was all intended to evoke a response from me. Well, it worked, but in hindsight, perhaps it wasn't so much him but the Spirit of God orchestrating events to bring us closer to finalizing the marriage. At that point, he had not filed the papers although he expressed his intent to divorce while I was still in Oklahoma.

I received my divorce papers right around Thanksgiving of 2010. Although I knew it was coming, it did not lessen the devastation that I felt when I received them. The devastation was replaced with an utter disgust, once he informed me that it would not be wise of me to dispute any of the contents which was basically telling me not to ask for anything. Well, what was there really to have, I thought? I left penniless, homeless and carless and you separated with the same thing you came into the marriage with; a job, a car and an apartment. I prayed about it and decided to send the papers back as quickly as possible so it would be over before the end of the year. That was my goal and his as well, to be free from this chapter of our lives and make a fresh start in the New Year. The only mistake that I made was not requesting to get my name back.

A few months passed and I was on the road again. I had taken the time to rest, with God and release myself from my horrific past. I took a step into the next leg of my journey by moving back to Florida, the place where it all started. I was excited about going back to Florida, which was always home for me. I didn't know what lay ahead of me, but I knew I was not going alone and I would be welcomed back with open arms. I remember the look on my mom's face when I asked her if I could come home. If you knew my mother, those were the sweetest words in her ears for any of her children. If she could have had us all in one house again, she would.

THE UNEXPRESSED VEIL

When I look back at that season of my life, I see clearly that everything I needed, (provision, covering and protection) God had always provided.

The favor of God has and will always be evident in my life no matter what I go through. Thank you Jesus for every wilderness experience and every ram in the bush. It was never God's intent for me to experience the things I went thru in my marriage, but it was something I had to go thru and I am all the better for it. It wasn't easy, but it was worth it for the wisdom, knowledge and intimate relationship that was restored with me and God.

The lesson in all of this is the understanding that our trials are allowed for the purpose of building character, faith and a greater dependence upon God. It's only in our trials that we find out who we really are and the depth of our real trust in God. It's not always going to be God's intent to deliver us from the trials, but to teach us in them.

I pray the things I've shared will not cause you to feel sorry for me, but rather to learn from me and draw strength in you.

From this experience, I learned that what God has put in me, will sustain me through any storm. "Greater is He that is in me than he that is in this world!" "I am more than a conqueror through Christ who strengthens me." To God be the glory!

CHAPTER 9
Welcome Back

When God led me back to Florida, to my mom's home, I finally had a sense of peace and purpose. I had been in communication with my mentor, Diana Lynn during the time of my separation and divorce. There was no way I could have survived that ordeal without her gentle and loving, spiritual guidance and wisdom. As she often did, she sent me an email with very encouraging words, some of which were prophetic, but what hit my spirit the most were the words she uttered in the beginning of the note, "Welcome back to the land of the living." Those words were so on point. God revealed many things to me about my husband after our divorce: (1) He was sent to distract me; (2) the assignment of the enemy was to silence my voice; (3) he was a counterfeit; and that; (4) he never loved me, ouch that hurt! My marriage had drained me of everything I felt was good in me, but God stepped in and refreshed me and breathed new life, giving me a second chance to re-discover my love for Him.

I recall Diana Lynn counseling me before I got married, to not lose myself in my marriage and that's exactly what I did. Everything about pleasing my husband. In hindsight, I wondered if perhaps she knew, by the Spirit, that I was about to take a wrong turn and just couldn't (by the Spirit) reveal that to me. Some things in life God strategically allows for His purpose to be fulfilled in us; unless a seed falls to the ground and dies it will not bear fruit. My Pastor teaches us that life is all about ***choices, decisions and consequences***. I made some unwise choices; I made decisions that I thought would please my flesh and I had to walk out the consequences of those decisions, but God had a plan that worked out for my good. I grew from every experience and I can say today that I'm grateful that God allowed it.

We are all responsible for our own choices. I could not and will never blame my husband for what I experienced. I take full responsibility for my part in the death of our marriage. I asked God for forgiveness; my husband for forgiveness and I'm learning to forgive myself. So now I am free to move forward in the new things God has for me. God gave me the time and opportunity to make peace with my past. Old things have passed away and all things have been made new. Thank you Jesus!

I learned a lot about myself while being married. My challenges revealed my flaws, weaknesses, vulnerability and how easily I could be swayed to compromise my faith. I also understood the effect our own hurt and pain can impact another person's life. Hurt people, hurt other people. What is in us will ultimately come out of us and sometimes only when we are shaken or when we experience turmoil. The enemy took full advantage of my husband's weakness and caused him to act outside of his character. My husband was a strong, loving and gentle soul who loved God and desired to please Him. Although, when faced with challenges beyond his control, he waivered in his faith and shut himself down and off from the people that loved him the most. He had become a master at deflecting his pain onto others rather than dealing with the issue until it was resolved.

The greatest lesson I learned in this season of my life was to know God's voice for yourself; take heed to the warnings that He gives you and always be perceptive and aware of the subtle tactics of the enemy to distract you from God's plan for your life. Yeah, I took a detour, but the road traveled was not in vain and I thank God for the lessons learned and His gentle way of bringing correction and ultimately restoring me to wholeness. A song that comes to mind as I recall this period in my life is, "I won't complain." That's my testimony: *"I've had some good days; I've had some hills to climb. I've had some weary days and sleepless nights. But when I look around and I think things over. All of my good days, outweigh my bad days and I won't complain"*.

CHAPTER 10
The Uncovering

God has revealed many valuable things to me in my season of isolation and for that I am grateful. Most importantly, I discovered my calling.

When that was revealed to me, I fully understood why I encountered such warfare in my life and marriage. My voice was going to be critical to my calling and God revealed to me that my husband had been used by the enemy to "steal my voice." Without a voice you cannot pray, prophesy nor teach and that is what God was calling me to do. God spoke to me in the middle of the night, "You MUST teach." I had never heard His voice as clearly as I did that night.

Not long after that, I was approached with a request to teach a children's ministry class. Knowing that I was called to teach, I saw that opportunity as confirmation. So as afraid as I was, I accepted the offer. I was determined I was going to give it my all, so I sought out resources and opportunities to learn more of God's word. My goal that year (2013-2014), was to become a student of the word. As God is always faithful to answer my prayers, he connected me to the most dynamic Bible teacher I've ever met, David Hill. He had just begun a bible study through our Church organization and was assisting with the newly developed discipleship class, Ministers in Training, (MIT). I was totally committed and was completely engaged in the weekly studies. He encouraged me simply by his passion to teach. I've never known anyone that seemed to get so much joy and pleasure out of sharing God's word. He has become a great mentor to me as I continue to pursue the same goal.

I spent more than a year under his guidance. The decision to pursue God opened up a door to me that I did not expect. It was of great honor and a complete surprise that I, as well as several other friends from my church, were called and ordained to be Ministers. God was positioning me and pushing me out of my nest which represented comfort, familiarity and safety. The day I was called to the altar, my Pastor prayed over me and the Spirit of God was upon me so strong I could barely stand. That was a moment that I will never forget, nor were the words he spoke to me by the Spirit. God said, "Freda, I've got your family!" Wow, those words breathed life into my spirit. I have for years prayed for my family members to be saved and that there would be no more premature deaths. God heard my hearts cry and was making it known to me.

In that same year, God revealed to me, through my mentor, that I would be a Prophetess, powerful intercessor and that my prayers would have power to change circumstances and outcomes. As she spoke the words, "Wow, God is really downloading on you today." I stood on God's word that if I prepare my heart, He would give me the words to speak. He is a God of His word!

It wasn't long after I was licensed as a Minister, that God began to give me opportunities to exercise and make full use of my gifts. I was excited, but still very unsure of my abilities, even though I knew He would not call me to anything He had not already equipped me to do. I was acting in His strength and not my own. God was teaching me to trust Him and have confidence within myself. I still have much to learn about being a prophetic voice and most of all, not doubting my ability to hear God's voice. Some days, that still remains a challenge for me, but not for long... I speak that over my life!

Lord, my eyes are now open and my ears are attentive to your voice. I won't go back to the way things used to be and I will never again allow Satan to steal my voice. I will pray, prophesy and teach. By your grace and mercy, I will Lead, Teach and Inspire others to live a lifestyle of obedience and to walk in victory. I will speak life and not death over my own life. I will live and NOT die and declare the works of the Lord. I will minister to ministers.

So you see, what I lost through my difficult seasons of life was nothing in comparison to what I gained spiritually. A restored relationship with the Lord and a hunger and thirst for God, peace and direction. To me these things are priceless. God said he was going to restore to me all that I had lost in the last seven years (2007-2014) and I have no doubt it will come to pass in His timing.

CHAPTER 11
Full Circle

"The steps of a good man are ordered by the Lord."

I always understood this scripture to mean only things that were in accordance with the will of God, which in my limited knowledge, was all "good things." Oh not so, God showed me that includes good and bad, because our destinies are in His hands. If He allows it, He has a purpose in it. God is a sovereign God. He knows each of us intimately and the plan that he has for us, therefore he knows exactly what must be done to develop us and get us to a place where He can use us for His Glory. We just have to hear his voice and run our race.

When I reflect on my life, the good, the bad and the UGLY, I can see the hand of God, the grace of God and the protection of God. The devil has tried to destroy me from the time I was a little girl, but God… does not allow the righteous to be moved.

What I know for sure, is that I have been kept by God! When Satan attacks you early in life, it's an indication that your assignment on the earth is BIG. Satan doesn't waste time on those that already belong to Him, but he relentlessly pursues those that God has chosen. I am a chosen one, Hallelujah!

My desire to know God began when I was just a young girl. I would sit and read for hours and although I had no understanding of what I read, something continued to draw me and give me a curiosity to know more. Reading became a means to escape the reality that was my life and it gave me a sense of safety and peace. Here I am many years later, many mistakes later, many disappointments later and I have returned to my first love.

My relationship with God has been inconsistent at times, but because of His great love for me, He always draws me back just like the prodigal son. I had to "come to myself" and allow God's love, mercy and forgiveness to restore me and bring me full circle. It is an awesome feeling to know that you are in the perfect will of God and the only thing that can break that circle is you. Again, as my Pastor says, "choices, decisions and consequences." I'd rather make right choices than deal with the consequence of a poor decision. Of course I realize I'm still on the potter's wheel so to speak and I will make mistakes, but I have a greater understanding of this process called Life.

So, those mistakes will be few and far between and if not, I know what God says, "A righteous man falls seven times but gets back up again." Lord, keep me from falling is all I can say. This is my season! I'm taking my life back and God is in complete control.

CHAPTER 12
The Launching

From Dream to Destiny... defines my current state in my walk with the Lord, "I am a rocket about to be launched into my purpose." It's time to give birth to my spiritual baby. The last two years have been a time of preparation, testing and cutting away. It's been painful, but necessary.

Only God knows the exact time of delivery. My responsibility is to fortify in this season and be prepared when He calls. Every prophetic word spoken over my life in the last two years, have been timely and a strategic move by God to make me aware of what is to come. The word says, "God does nothing unless He first reveals it to His Prophets."

I know the things God has entrusted to me are in His timing based on what He knew I could handle, without running from it. If God had shown me, years ago, what I'm currently doing in serving His people, I would have been scared out of my mind and I'd look for any and every excuse in the world not to comply.

God has been in control of every season and aspect of my life. I know there has been great purpose for every individual he allowed to be part of my journey. After having survived so much turmoil in my marriage, it was time for me to get back on track. God had just the right person in mind to help me get my fire back and her name was Diana Lynn Gaddey. She is my spiritual mentor that I have mentioned multiple times.

Diana Lynn has always been a prophetic voice, a trusted friend and confidant through the years. When she moved from the area, many of the young ladies she mentored, (myself included) felt a sense of loss and separation, but waited patiently for the day when God would release her into her ministry. After years of a God directed season of hibernation in Minnesota, God led each of us back to her, even though we were scattered among many states. God was up to something and it was BIG! He was about to birth the ministry of "Destiny's Calling". A ministry focused on finding, preparing and launching women into their God assigned purpose. I was so excited to receive the invitation to join her in the launching of this ministry.

God had a plan for her life and we were to be part of that plan - knitted and woven together like a fine tapestry. Each thread being an integral part of the design. As I serve alongside her, God is showing me, what I need to do in preparation for the launching of my own ministry. In the process, I have seen God move mightily. Just as we previously experienced as a group in what we called "the upper room", at our former church. The Holy Spirit shows up every time we come together. Monday night conference calls are our appointed time with Him and He never disappoints. God's love for the ladies in this group has been so amazing. There is a wealth of talent and gifts amongst us and she encourages every one of us to flow in those gifts, knowing that we are in a safe place to test them out.

Our first Women's Retreat was a great success in 2014. We were amazed as usual to see God move in the lives of so many of the women. We witnessed supernatural moves of God that we will all be talking about for years to come.

God spoke to us during the planning process of the first Destiny's Calling Ministry Retreat that this would be the launching pad for all of us into our individual ministries. I believe that process has begun. I know it has for me.

Since the conference, I have been ministering and God has connected me to women that will no doubt take part in future conferences or perhaps be supporters of the ministry that will be birthed through me.

I don't know the full scope and I don't need to. I'm just being obedient to move when He says move and go, when He says go.

It is now February 2016. God spoke in 2014 that he was going to anoint me to write my book over the next twelve months. The delay has been my own doing. Again, you could have never told me that I would write a book. That was a part of God's plan and I received it and I completed the first draft in that time frame in 2015. I already know there are multiple books to be birthed. I had so many delays and distractions during the writing process. I knew it would be birthed through tears, anguish and sorrow. I've never given birth in the natural, but this book alone has allowed me to experience the process of the pain, discomfort and stretching that comes with the natural birthing process. This is my baby.

CHAPTER 13
The Unexpected Ending

While writing this book, my mother was diagnosed with bladder cancer and kidney failure.

Mama began to look frail and weak, which was unusual for us to see. We were very concerned, but as always, she never complained about feeling bad and always responded to our inquiries with "I'm okay." After seeing changes in her behavior and mental capacity, it was soon revealed that there was a problem and it was very serious. My sister, Amber noticed she was bleeding heavily and called it to my attention. She hated being confronted or told what to do, but this time, we had no choice. When she got up to go to her room, we followed her after seeing the blood. She became nervous and agitated when we asked her about it. She denied anything was wrong. We ended up calling the paramedics and thank God we did. Her blood pressure was dangerously low, and after constant badgering from us, as well as the paramedics telling her she would bleed to death if she didn't seek treatment, she agreed to go to the hospital.

She obviously knew she was sick but didn't want us to know. With much fear in her eyes, I rode with her to keep her calm. After many tests, the doctors informed us that she had bladder cancer, an aneurysm, kidney failure and had suffered a mild heart attack at some point. She stayed in the hospital long enough for them to put a stint in her bladder, which would give her 30% kidney function, so she could go home. That was her desire. She adamantly refused all other treatments that may or may not have sustained her life.

During her illness, we saw a side to mama that we had never witnessed before. She was more at peace and fun loving and that made the ordeal for us so much more bearable. Mama lived much longer than the doctors told us she would and I know that was by God's design. After watching her for months, I knew God was taking her through a time of emotional healing, forgiveness and giving her time to make peace and let go of things that had for years weighed her down in her spirit. My mother was saved and I knew she loved the Lord, so I never had a concern about where she would spend eternity. Through her illness, I prayed that He would not allow her to suffer with pain or when the time came, to be aware of her transition and lastly, that her children would be with her when that time came.

I shared, with my sister Carolyn, how much it meant to mama to have her come home and be there for her. There had always been tension between them, since Carolyn was a young girl, stemming from things that happened in her own childhood. That was THE area that I believe caused my mom the most sadness, but God did a work in both of them during her illness and brought peace and reconciliation to both.

I was sitting in my mom's room one day and she had this faraway look in her eyes. I watched her for a long time and finally asked, "What are you thinking about?" Normally her response would always be nothing. This time, to my utter shock she just started talking.

With every word she spoke, I felt like I was getting to know my mother for the first time and I was intrigued by what she shared. My heart was so saddened by what she spoke and I wished, at that moment, that I could have wiped away all that sadness. Her life, her actions, her moods began to make sense to me. She said she felt better after we talked and she looked lighter; like a weight had been lifted from her. I knew God had intervened and I quickly grabbed a notebook and wrote down everything she shared. I wanted to always remember that moment.

To look at my mom, you would never have known she was as ill as she was. She bounced back after being in the hospital. It was almost a year before she started showing signs of sickness again. My sister, Amber quit her job to take care of my mom full-time. That was a blessing to them both. As much as they argued, mama was relieved and happy to have her with her every day. Eventually she suffered a couple of mini strokes while under hospice care and that was the beginning of the end. She became withdrawn, quiet, and weak and she had begun to lose her appetite.

I think she withdrew because she hated and never

wanted to get to a point in her life where her children had to care for her to the extent we did. She never wanted to be a burden and no matter what we said to convince her, that's how she felt. She had become so frail at this point, we had to lift her whenever she wanted to sit in her chair or go to the bathroom. Once, while we were preparing to change the bed linens, she looked up at Amber and I and said, "Aren't you tired of me yet?" It was shocking to us to see how quickly her physical body had changed in size. It was just heart-wrenching to see our mother like this. It was a site that will always remain in my mind.

Some of the family from Virginia visited mama during her time of illness, which she enjoyed so much. She was particularly excited when her grandson, Brandon, who is an aspiring puppeteer came down for the summer. I'd never seen her laugh so much at his performances.

Brandon, I want to personally thank you for making her last days so full of joy and pleasure. Before she became lethargic, my brother Freddie came to visit with her. He got her to sit up and go outside, which she had always enjoyed. It was like an awakening in her. One morning, he had her sitting up in her chair listening to Al Green songs. Al was her favorite. As she always did in response to a good song whether secular or Christian, she closed her eyes and rocked back and forth. This was a good day! When Freddie left, he promised her he would come back again to visit and bring the kids.

The last time I saw my mom with her eyes open was on my birthday, January 25, 2015. I came into her room to get ready for church, and Amber was sitting by her bedside, as was her daily routine. I leaned down to kiss her. Her eyes appeared to be closed shut. Amber said, "Hey granny its auntie's birthday today…" and she opened her eyes briefly, but I saw no life there. While I was dressing, Carolyn called to speak with her. She told Amber to hold the phone to mom's ear while she spoke. I turned my attention to the words she was speaking. I broke down in tears and ran into my closet to ensure mama didn't hear me. My mom's eyes were closed, but she began to cry as well. This was the final stage in both their healings. Carolyn asked her to forgive her for any pain she had caused her. She told her she now understood all the things she went through as a wife and mother. She thanked her for being the best mom she could be and her final words were letting her know she could go and we would all be alright.

As promised, on Wednesday, January 28th, Freddie came back with his son Brandon, daughter Stephanie and to our surprise, my sister, Carolyn. When they got there, mama was in and out of consciousness, but I knew she could hear their voices even if she didn't respond as she normally would. She knew they were there. As excited as I was, I instantly felt like it was not a coincidence that Freddie and Carolyn where there. It wasn't! God had completely orchestrated this visit.

That night, we all stayed close to her, just watching

her. Stephanie sat at her bedside, held her hands and sang softly in her ear the Little Mermaid song, which mama always asked her to sing. We were all getting a little tired and restless, so we found things to take our minds off the situation. Amber remained in the room with her. In the middle of the night, I heard her yell out. Mama had started coughing up blood. When I got into the room, Amber was holding her, but was visibly shaken and afraid of what she was witnessing, and through her tears, she told me that she couldn't do this. I grabbed mama and held her in my arms. She never opened her eyes or said a word through the entire experience. She seemed limp but I held her so she would not choke on the blood. We immediately called hospice. They came out within hours. By that time, she was at ease but seemed agitated and her breathing was somewhat labored. Again, she never opened her eyes or spoke. They arrived and gave her an examination, and told us it would not be long. Perhaps another day but no more. I had no words at that reality, nor did anyone else. We wanted her to be comfortable and after they gave her some medication, her body appeared to be at rest.

The next day, January 29th 2015, around 7:00 A.M., I heard Freddie say, "She's gone". The screaming through the house was bone chilling. Mama had quietly and peacefully transitioned into the presence of the Lord, while Carolyn lay asleep in the chair next to her bed. She was finally free from the troubles of this world. Every time I hear this song in my spirit, I can imagine mama saying:

Soon I will be done
with the troubles of the world
Troubles of the world
Troubles of the world
Soon I will be done
Troubles of the world
I'm going home to live with my Lord

By Mahalia Jackson

After all of us having been in the room with her the night before, she passed away while we were all asleep. Perhaps that was God's intent. We all knew from the events of the night before that it was going to be soon, but it did not prevent the unbelievable shock and pain we all felt when we heard Freddie say the words, "She's gone!" I'm so glad I got the opportunity to hold her in my arms early that morning before she passed, even though she probably didn't know.

The depth of my pain in the loss of my mother was greater than I could have imagined. My peace came in knowing that God answered my prayers for her. She just went to sleep, with her family around her and no conscious awareness, I believe, of her passing. Thank you, Jesus.

I was engaged in a conversation recently regarding leaving a legacy for your family. As I listened to others share about financial legacies, my initial thought was that we had not been left a legacy. Yet, the Holy Spirit clarified that for me. Some may understand a legacy in terms of financial blessing.

For our family, the legacy mama left for all of us was LOVE! The value and importance she placed on giving and receiving love. The greatest of all legacies given to us by our parents was a biblical foundation of Knowing God. How awesome is that!

This book is my personal testimony and reflection of my journey with the Lord, while discovering who I am in Christ, to this point. I believe something happened to my siblings in mama's death. I believe we all felt a sense of loss in being disconnected from the one that had given birth to us. A deep feeling of loss and inability to communicate or deal with the pain that we each were feeling. We were like lost pups. The one person that kept us all together was now gone.

At 51 years old, I'm grateful for the grace and mercy of God to preserve me for such a time as this. I can attest to the word of the Lord that we have angels all around us. My angel has always been on assignment. I'm honored that the Holy Spirit anointed me to write this book. I got my voice back and I will never be silenced again, no matter how many attacks the enemy throws at me. I believe my story will be used to bring light, hope and healing to all those that read it. I assure you that by God's grace and mercy, I look nothing like what I've been through.

I leave you with these insightful nuggets of wisdom that I have learned along the way. I hope that they will guide you in your daily life, relationships and your walk with the Lord. I pray that it will help you navigate your way through the traps and pitfalls that the enemy will surely try to stop you with.

• Know the voice of the Holy Spirit for yourself (my sheep know my voice and no other voice will they follow).

• Right things done out of order bring disastrous results. Trust in God's timing!

• What does not kill you, makes you stronger.

• Don't neglect to communicate what's in your heart. Your words could be the catalyst to changing someone else's life, circumstance or situation. Silence is not always golden.

• Sometimes, what we perceive as God taking something from us is really God's way of protecting us and preserving us for something better.

• Don't hold on to your pain; allow yourself to feel and experience the pain so you can heal and move on.

• Weeping may endure for a night, but joy comes in the morning.

• Always take responsibility for your own actions; don't deflect your issues onto others.

• Open your mouth!

I don't know what's next for me, but I do know God has preordained every step. I know today that I am loved. I know that I am worthy. I know my destiny awaits me and the spiritual birthing is about to take place. I know that I have favor with the Lord and every trial was to strengthen me, teach me and develop me into a Mighty Woman of God. *I wouldn't take nothing for my journey now. – Maya Angelou*

A friend of mine shared this on Social Media and I knew instantly it was a word for me. So, as she spoke into my life, I speak into yours with this excerpt:

"The Lord showed me a vision of a woman giving birth, and the moment the baby's head crowned, she shut her legs tight. The Lord said, tell the woman "Don't kill your promise because you're afraid to push! If this is for you, Push Mama Push! Push till you get your breakthrough! Push till you see a change! Push till God answers you! Push till God shows up on your behalf! He impregnated you with the promise so He's faithful enough to coach you THROUGH the process to deliver the promise." - Latisha Davis

Made in the USA
Middletown, DE
27 January 2021